A Beautiful Way of Living

The Meditation Teachings of Godwin Samararatne

Edited and compiled by
Dennis Candy and
Sampath Dissanayake

Foreword by Bhikkhu Bodhi

Buddhist Publication Society
P.O. Box 61, 54, Sangharaja Mawatha
Kandy, Sri Lanka

Copyright © 2011 Nilambe Buddhist Meditation Centre Trust Board.

First Edition: 2011

Extracts from this book may be reproduced without permission provided acknowledgement is given to the editors and publisher.

The talks by Godwin Samaratne in this book have been compiled and re-edited with permission from texts published on www.godwin-home-page.net edited and copyrighted by Jeanne Mynett from the original transcripts

National Library and Documentation Centre - Cataloguing-in-Publication (CIP) Data

---

Samararatne, Godwin
  A Beautiful Way of Living: The Meditation Teachings of Godwin Samararatne / Godwin Samararatne.- Kandy: Buddhist Publication Society Inc. 2010.
  BP 430S. - 194p.; 22cm.

  ISBN 978-955-24-0358-3

  i. 294.34432 DDC 22   ii. Title
  1. Meditation - Buddhism

ISBN 978-955-24-0358-3

Typeset at the BPS in UtopiaBPS

Printed by
Ruchira Offset Printers
Kandy—Sri Lanka

Contents

Foreword v
Introduction ix

Part One: About Meditation

1. Why Meditate? ... 3
2. Meditation on Breathing ... 12
3. Developing a Skilful Approach to Meditation ... 22
4. Loving-kindness Meditation ... 26
5. Sharing Our Experiences of Meditation ... 33
6. Observing Our Thoughts ... 39
7. Meditation Problems ... 55
8. A Mind Like a Mirror ... 61

Part Two: Practice in Daily Life

9. Working with Emotions ... 71
10. How We Create Suffering: Giving Plusses and Minuses ... 85
11. Developing Loving-kindness ... 98
12. A Spiritual Approach to Friendship ... 117
13. Problems of Everyday Life ... 127
14. Integrating Meditation with Everyday Life ... 133
15. The Importance of Awareness ... 155

Part Three: The Importance of the Buddha's Teachings

16. The Four Noble Truths and Liberation from Suffering ... 163
17. The Importance of the Dhamma in the Modern World ... 172

Foreword

As a predominantly Theravada Buddhist country, Sri Lanka has secured its place in the international Buddhist arena primarily through its distinguished monastic order, which has included some of the most erudite and eloquent monks of the modern world. However, in addition to its monks, Sri Lanka can also boast of a corps of outstanding lay Buddhist teachers who have achieved international renown as scholars, thinkers, preachers, and spiritual guides. Among these are Anagarika Dharmapala, who spearheaded the Buddhist revival in the late nineteenth and early twentieth centuries; the Buddhist scholars G.P. Malalasekera, O.H. de A. Wijesekera, and Lily De Silva; the philosophers K.N. Jayatilleke, David Kalupahana, Y. Karunadasa, and P.D. Premasiri; and the social activist and proponent of peace, A.T. Ariyaratne, founder of the Sarvodaya Shramadana movement.

Belonging to this same current of eminent lay teachers was a quiet, thoughtful, and serene resident of Kandy named Godwin Samararatne, with whom I had the fortune to be closely associated during my twenty-three years living in Sri Lanka. I first met Godwin within two months of my arrival in Sri Lanka, in late 1972, when I was visiting the great German elder Ven. Nyanaponika at the Forest Hermitage. At the time, Godwin was working as librarian at the Kandy Municipal Library, but his keen interest in Buddhism, psychology, and human spirituality often drew him to the Forest Hermitage to borrow books and discuss ideas with Ven. Nyanaponika. It was Ven. Nyanaponika's books, *The Heart of Buddhist Meditation* and *The Power of Mindfulness*, that inspired Godwin to take up the practice of meditation. Within a decade his commitment to the practice had become so serious that he left his job as librarian to become a full-time meditator, then a local meditation teacher, and finally an international meditation teacher.

For close to twenty years, Godwin had been the resident teacher at the Nilambe Meditation Centre in the lovely Sri Lankan hill country. He had also taught meditation at the Lewella and Visakha Meditation Centres (two affiliates of Nilambe), in Kandy itself at the University of Peradeniya, at private homes, and at the Buddhist Publication Society. But Godwin did not belong to Sri Lanka alone. He belonged to the whole world, and he was loved and esteemed by people around the globe. Thousands of people from many lands came to Nilambe to practise under his guidance, and they also invited him to their own countries to conduct meditation courses and retreats. Thus for over two decades Godwin had become an international Buddhist figure, constantly in demand in countries ranging from Europe to Singapore and Hong Kong. He was also a regular visitor to South Africa, where he conducted his last meditation retreat just months before his death.

What was so impressive about Godwin was not what he did but what he was. I can say that Godwin was above all a truly selfless person, and it was this utter selflessness of the man that accounts for the impact he had on the lives of so many people. I use the word "selflessness" to describe Godwin in two interrelated senses. First, he was selfless in the sense that he seemed to have almost no inner gravitational force of a self around which his personal life revolved: no pride, no ambition, no personal projects aimed at self-aggrandizement. He was humble and non-assertive, not in an artificial self-demeaning way, but as if he had no awareness of a self to be effaced. Hence as a meditation teacher he could be utterly transparent, without any trips of his own to lay on his students.

This inward "emptiness" enabled Godwin to be selfless in the second sense: as one who always gave first consideration to the welfare of others. He empathized with others and shared their concerns as vividly as if they were his own. In this respect, Godwin embodied the twin Buddhist virtues of loving-kindness and compassion, *mettā* and *karunā*. Even without many words, his dignified presence conveyed a quietude and calm that spoke eloquently for the power of inner goodness, for its capacity to reach out to others and heal their anxiety and distress. It was this deep quietude and almost tangible kindness that drew thousands of people to Godwin and encouraged them to welcome him into their lives. The trust they placed in him was well deposited, for in an age when so many popular "gurus" have gained notoriety for their unscrupulous behaviour, he never exploited the confidence and good will of his pupils.

Though Godwin taught the practice of Buddhist meditation, particularly the "way of mindfulness," he did not try to propagate "Buddhism" as a doctrine or religious faith, much less as part of an exotic cultural package. His inspiration came from the Dhamma as a path of inner transformation whose effectiveness stemmed primarily from its ability to promote self-knowledge and self-purification. He saw the practice of meditation as a way to help people help themselves, to understand themselves better and change themselves for the better. He emphasized that Buddhist meditation is not a way of withdrawing from everyday life, but of living everyday life mindfully, with awareness and clear comprehension, and he taught people how to apply the Dhamma to the knottiest problems of their personal lives.

By not binding the practice of meditation to the traditional religious framework of Buddhism, Godwin was able to reach out and speak to people of the most diverse backgrounds. For him there were no essential, unbridgeable differences between human beings. He saw people everywhere as just human beings beset by suffering and searching for happiness, and he offered the Buddha's practice of mindfulness as an experiential discipline leading to genuine peace of heart. Hence he could teach people from such different backgrounds—Western, Asian, and African; Buddhist, Hindu, Christian, and Muslim; Sri Lankan Theravadins and Chinese Mahayanists—and all could respond readily to his guidance. If it was not for a chronic liver condition that he had patiently endured for years, with hardly a word of complaint, Godwin might well have lived on to actively teach the way of mindfulness for at least another decade. But this was not to be, for in late February of the year 2000, almost immediately upon his return from a teaching engagement in South Africa, his illness deteriorated and a month later claimed his precious life.

It is an act of merit that several of his students and Dhamma friends have decided to collect a number of his discourses into a single volume. This will help to keep alive the legacy of this gentle ambassador of the Dhamma.

Bhikkhu Bodhi,
Chuang Yen Monastery,
Carmel, New York, USA

INTRODUCTION

For more than 20 years until his death in March 2000 at the age of sixty-eight Godwin Samararatne devoted his life to teaching meditation principally at the Nilambe Meditation Centre near Kandy but also at other places around the world. During his lifetime he became a highly regarded teacher of meditation and thousands of people from many countries benefitted from his teachings. One of the main reasons for Godwin's high reputation is that he had the wonderful ability to use familiar, everyday language and experiences in order to explain the healing benefits of Buddhist meditation and the Dhamma and to relate these to the events and experiences of daily life.

Godwin himself taught people directly and did not write about his own approach to meditation. But since his death there has been continued and growing interest in his teachings. This has been marked by the setting up of an internet website (www.godwin-home-page.net) by the British bhikkhu Venerable Anandajoti containing recordings and transcripts of a large number of Godwin's talks, as well as other relevant material. In addition, several books and pamphlets comprising transcripts of some of his talks, and details about his teachings, have been published in Asia and in the USA.

These publications are of great benefit to those who attended Godwin's talks and retreats because they enable them to refresh their memories about his approach to meditation. But the wider availability of these records has also led to a large number of people who never personally encountered Godwin to want to learn more about this remarkable teacher. It therefore seems timely to mark 10 years since Godwin's passing by producing a book about his teachings and the beneficial effect they have had on a wide range of people.

In undertaking this task we have tried to present Godwin's mature teachings in his own words on the practical aspects of Buddhist meditation and the Dhamma. To do this we have utilised extracts from talks that Godwin gave in a number of different locations and then put them together to try to fashion a coherent structure in which he explains and talks about his principal themes and ideas regarding meditation and the Dhamma.

Although we have made an attempt to put the talks into a structure, each chapter is self-contained and they can be fruitfully read and pondered upon in any order that the reader wishes. They have been selected and put together from transcripts of recordings made during retreats and discussions in various countries during the 1990s and subsequently made available on the Godwin-Home-Page website. We have carried out further editing of the texts to aid in the sequencing of the talks and discussions and to eliminate repetitions.

The book is very much intended as an aid to the practice of meditation and as guidance for anyone working towards understanding and freeing themselves from suffering (*dukkha*). Therefore the talks and discussions included in it have been selected primarily because they explain the use of simple, practical, meditative 'tools' or approaches that we can use in the circumstances of our own lives and that can bring definite benefits. Godwin always encouraged people to see meditation as something that is directly relevant to their day-to-day lives and their ordinary human mind and its operations. By applying right mindfulness or awareness (*sati*) to all the experiences of life we can begin the process of what his friend Nyanaponika Thera often described as knowing the mind, shaping the mind and freeing the mind, a description of meditation which Godwin frequently quoted in his own talks.

Godwin argued that through the application of right mindfulness in daily activities we can become aware of the shallowness, limitations and psychological pain associated with strongly identifying with 'I' and 'mine'. This discipline of mindfulness helps us to experience psychological freedom from the suffering that arises due to attachment to these mental constructs and helps to provide us with the means to use them skilfully in our ordinary practical lives by knowing the limitations of their usage and application.

To help us Godwin developed his own unique way of explaining the benefits of meditation and mindfulness by the use of simple tools and methods. He combined this with open discussions with meditators about their personal experiences of the nature and workings of the human mind and body. He then used these discussions to help guide us towards a deeper understanding of our discontent and mental suffering and how to overcome it and suggested ways in which we can experience the emergence of wholesome joy in our lives.

Godwin had made the effort to understand the deep practical truths of the Buddha's teachings, especially in relation to meditation. He had also studied and tried to apply the insights of other spiritual teachers from Asia, such as J. Krishnamurti and Ramana Maharshi, as well as therapists and counsellors, such as Carl Rogers, Gustav Jung and Daniel Goleman, from Western traditions. He skilfully used what he learnt from these sources to develop his understanding and his teaching skills. As a result he developed a wide practical experience as a counsellor and therapist who was able to work with people from both Asian and Western cultural backgrounds and to advise Western-trained psychiatrists in Sri Lanka.

Through deep reflection over many years on the experience of his own meditation practice and that of others and his deep compassion for the distress of others, Godwin became highly skilled at applying the Buddha's Four Noble Truths to the everyday experiences of suffering that ordinary people have. In particular, he realised that much of the suffering of the Western people he encountered took the form of intense dislike for certain aspects of themselves or their families. This seemed to be related to their upbringing in the highly competitive and judgmental social systems that have evolved in the West.

For example, popular and dominant values in the West put great emphasis from an early age on ideals such as being materially and educationally 'successful', having a 'perfect' body, owning the latest designer-label possessions, and so on. Or, as the popular phraseology puts it, being a 'winner' rather than a 'loser'. Inevitably, with such an unrealistic set of aspirations, most people cannot achieve these ideals. As a result, and in the absence of a deeper appreciation of other factors (such as kamma) which affect the course of their lives, they can become beset by thoughts of personal inadequacy, inferiority and similar negative feelings about themselves or their families. These negative feelings often begin at an early age, even at pre-school level.

Over time these oppressive, negative mental states can lead those who experience them to prolonged periods of unhappiness and depression. Or they may rebel against their parents, teachers and society for making unrealistic demands on them and develop deep antagonism towards their parents or society for creating their problems. Either way it leads to intense conflict and psychological suffering—dukkha.

Godwin saw that meditation and the Dhamma could be applied to help people free themselves from the distress that can arise from these aspects of life in the modern world, just as much as they can be used for helping those affected by the more traditional forms of suffering. Taking inspiration from the timeless teachings in the Buddhist scriptures, and from other sources as well, he used his own compassionate and penetrative insights into the origins of suffering to develop a series of what he called "tools" to help people reduce and even free themselves from the experience of mental distress, or dukkha. It is the explanation and practical application of these tools that form the heart of Godwin's approach to meditation and that we have tried to present in this book.

We would like to thank Bhante Ānandajoti, the webmaster of the Godwin-Home-Page website, and Ms. Jeanne Mynett, the website's editor, for permission to use extensive extracts from the talks by Godwin made available on that website and for helpful suggestions to improve the book. Those extracts, edited by Ms Mynett from the original transcripts, have been further edited and restructured by us and we take sole responsibility for the final form in which they appear here. We also wish to extend thanks to our Dhamma friends in Hong Kong, Singapore, South Africa and a number of European countries who spent many hours patiently transcribing the talks and discussions from the original taped recordings. Without their work, this book would not have been possible.

Dennis Candy and Sampath Dissanayake,
Compilers and Editors

Part One

About Meditation

1
WHY MEDITATE?

The question is why should we meditate? What is the importance of meditation? Why is it emphasised so much in the Buddha's teaching? These are some of the questions that I'm going to explore in my talk.

The word meditation translates the Pali word *bhāvāna* which means cultivating the mind, developing the mind, mental culture. So the whole emphasis is on the mind. When you read the Buddhist texts you are so amazed at the Buddha's profound and deep statements about the human mind. It is amazing that he should have made these statements 2,600 years ago. In fact, modern psychologists and psychotherapists are also deeply inspired by the Buddha's statements on the human mind.

The idea of meditation has been expressed by Nyanaponika Thera in these terms: knowing the mind, shaping the mind, and freeing the mind. I would like to repeat the words: meditation is knowing the mind, shaping the mind, and freeing the mind. Knowing the mind is understanding how the mind is working. If we do not know our mind we are really just like machines. Therefore it is extremely important to know and to understand how our minds work.

And when we know the mind, then we can shape the mind. Shaping the mind is developing mastery over the mind. If we do not develop mastery over the mind what happens is that we become a slave to our own mind. When we become slaves to our mind, then thoughts and emotions control us, and that results in more and more suffering. Therefore it is very important to learn to shape the mind, and when you learn to shape the mind then you can achieve a mind that is free. So the importance of meditation is learning to achieve a mind that is free, a mind that is happy, a mind that is peaceful, a mind that has loving-kindness.

HEALING THE MIND

It is interesting to see the things we do to keep our body healthy. We feed our body, we keep the body clean. When the body becomes sick we go to the doctor and get medicine to cure the illnesses. We do so many things to keep the body healthy. An interesting question is: what do we do to keep our mind healthy? Have you given thought to this very important question? We have to be clear about what makes our mind sick, what makes our mind unhealthy.

What are the symptoms of the human sicknesses of the mind? Meditation is learning about them and achieving a mind that is completely healthy. We can consider some emotions as contributing to the illnesses of the human mind. I would like to mention some of these emotions, and I'm sure everyone here can relate to them: anxiety, stress, fear, insecurity, and sadness. I can draw up a long list, which I think we can all relate to.

Sometimes we don't realise that they make our mind sick. If we do not know that they can create our sickness we can continue to have that sickness without finding a solution to it. In one of my talks I will be speaking about emotions and I will present to you how meditation helps us to work with emotions. When I speak about emotions I will be interested to hear from you what emotions really bother you in this country. So I will be presenting some practical ways of working with these unpleasant emotions and then finding a way to be free from these emotions.

Another very important aspect of meditation is that meditation helps us to experience with full awareness things that arise. There are some who know very well what the Buddha taught, so they are very knowledgeable about Buddhism. But they have not experienced directly anything from the Buddha's teaching because they have not meditated. They are like people who know all about meals but they have hardly tasted the food from the meals. So meditation helps us to taste; and when you have tasted it you achieve a kind of appetite for the freedom of the mind. When you taste it, you really see for yourself how we can free ourselves.

Related to this is another point: that meditation helps us to become completely self-reliant. When you meditate you realise that you have to take responsibility for what is happening in your mind. Sometimes I define meditation in my own words as finding the medicine for the sickness we have created ourselves. As we create the sickness ourselves, we have to find the medicine.

When you are sick, if you want to heal yourself you cannot tell others to take the medicine. The Buddha emphasised this point very much: to be self-reliant, to rely on one's own efforts. The Buddha said self-effort is the best effort. And when we develop self-effort, when we become self-reliant, then what happens is we learn to become completely self-confident about ourselves. When we have this self-confidence, when we see for ourselves that the medicine is helping, then that gives us more confidence in the medicine and it also helps us to develop faith and confidence in the person who discovered the medicine.

Meditation as Exploration

Another thing, when we look at our minds, is to see how our perceptions give rise to our conceptions—and how our conceptions can alter our perceptions also. In addition, we have to look at our bodies and sensations, how we relate to them, and what is the connection between the body and the mind. Take, for example, the question of physical pain. Normally what do we do if there is physical pain? If we are sitting on the benches here, and after a time pain arises, we move. Why? Because we don't like it. But by that response do we ever learn anything about pain? We just react in a very conditioned way. Now in meditation one tries to learn about pain, we try not to have that immediate, habitual, reaction. We might learn that physical pain gives rise to various psychological states—dislike, fear, anxiety, and so forth. So then we might try to see if it's possible to have this physical pain without having the psychological reaction.

Related to pain, of course, is pleasure. We like pleasurable sensations to continue, and painful ones to stop. But in meditation we realise that what happens is often quite contrary to what we want. By wanting certain sensations to continue, conflict arises, because we have made a projection of how we want the world to be. But when the world doesn't live up to our expectations, then there is conflict.

Another area to try to explore in meditation is our relationships with other people and with the world. Most of our problems and conflicts, as well as our joys and happiness, derive from our relationships: the way we relate to ourselves and to our environment. In meditation one learns to understand these relationships, and through that to learn about ourselves.

Also, our emotions are an important area to inquire into. Now normally when we are angry, for instance, we are just angry, with no consciousness of how that anger is affecting our body, or what psychological complexes it gives rise to. With someone who is not a meditator, if we ask them: Why are you getting angry? invariably we get the response that the other person is responsible, that they have provoked the anger. Now it is a very important aspect of meditation that one learns to take responsibility for what is happening in one's own mind, that we learn to no longer blame others—because that is the easy way out, if they are to blame you don't have to do anything about it.

This brings up the point that we create a world of our own, from our conclusions, prejudices, expectations, and conditionings. Anything that does not correspond to this private world we have constructed gives rise to suffering and conflict. In meditation we come to understand this process; then we can learn that problems are mainly in relation to one's own conclusions about how the world should be. To put it another way, we realise that a lot of what we are seeing is subjective, and then we try to see how that subjectivity operates. Gradually we see how far we can become objective, learning to see things as they are, not as they should or must be.

* * *

Discussion

I would now like to discuss with you how we can find meditation interesting, how we can sometimes find it entertaining, a little amusing, how we can develop a taste for it, how we can develop a curiosity about meditation.

Let us see what happens. I will start and tell you how I find my thoughts interesting. With my thoughts sometimes I suddenly find myself back in Sri Lanka! It only takes a few seconds and I can visit any country in the world I like, and without a visa! Isn't that interesting? Just watching this is fascinating. This is only one example. Are your thoughts like that?

Retreatant: I not only go to other countries but I am connected with so many people who are important to me, who are interesting, whom I like.

Godwin: Exactly. So even without the people being here we can meet them, and sometimes we have dialogues with them, sometimes arguments, and here we can even start a new argument. The argument was old but here you can start it again anew, thinking: I should have said that, too! Or, if he or she says that, I could say this, and he would be silenced! This is the way to find it amusing, this is the way to find it entertaining. So today, what I said was just to watch what is happening. This is a big challenge.

Retreatant: I do not need to meditate for this, I do this all of the time.

Godwin: You are an excellent meditator then! Today I was emphasising awareness, alertness, being awake, that is the difference.

Daydreaming

Retreatant: The examples you have given so far, it sounds more like daydreaming to me, and not what I understand meditation to be all about, which is that we are trying hard to get away from our thoughts, for the mind to settle for a second—I think the examples you are giving are not what I understood meditation to be about.

❈ **Godwin:** I am not surprised to hear this. But if you are daydreaming, you can never be alert and awake. And if you are not alert and awake you will not know what thoughts are arising, as I have said quite a few times. Can you be aware of each thought that arises? That needs a lot of space, a lot of clarity. If you are daydreaming you cannot do that.

In subsequent discussions I hope to speak about the stories that we construct, the daydreaming and fantasies, and to even explore questions like: what is the difference between a daydream and a night-dream? Very interesting material.

Then, there is another very fascinating thing we do, especially with our thoughts. From the time that we wake up in the morning to the time that we go to sleep, generally speaking we have this continuous chattering going through our minds. Let us be honest—while you are listening to me you have your own inner chattering going on.

So an interesting question is: what are we thinking about from the time we get up in the morning until the time we go to sleep? What are the themes? You see the importance of observing thoughts? What are you thinking now?

❧ **Retreatant:** I think I have no idea what I was thinking of!

❈ **Godwin:** I am not surprised, that seems to be a reaction of most of the people here. Please consider this as a meditation, reflecting on the themes of our thoughts, the contents of our thoughts.

BEING OPEN TO THE UNEXPECTED

❧ **Retreatant:** For me it is interesting to see how thoughts and emotions just arise, without my influencing it.

❈ **Godwin:** To put it in another way: we realise that we have no control. Today I felt that during the day some of you were experiencing boredom. I felt that some of you were feeling very tired, I felt that some of you were feeling very restless, I felt some of you were feeling a little confused. So this is the meditation! As a Zen master said: there is no escape.

Without escaping from such feelings what we are doing is learning from them, discovering about them, finding out about them. Otherwise what happens in everyday life is that these moods, these emotions, they come and go, and we really do not know the mechanism of how they are operating. We normally become passive victims of this process, or we try to escape from them. Does that work? But here in meditation we learn to confront these emotions, to be with them. Aren't we meeting a real challenge in life?

This is why meditators are called warriors. There are two types of warriors. One type is *worriers*! But there is another type of warrior where they have the courage, they have the confidence to be a warrior, and to work with these difficult emotions, to play with them. So this is what we will be doing during the next few days, practising to become more and more like warriors in the second sense of the word.

I am just reminded of something that happened in the meditation centre at Nilambe—it could never happen here. One evening we discussed the importance of being warriors. Then afterwards the meditators went to their rooms to sleep, and one of the women heard a big noise outside her room. She opened the door and she saw a huge buffalo outside. Naturally there was fear, there was anxiety, insecurity; there was panic coming up. Fortunately, she thought of the evening discussion we had just had, and she asked herself: How can I be a warrior now? And she said that something amazing happened—it was so inspiring—how when she thought of being a warrior there was simply no problem. So meditation helps us to work with buffaloes! Shouldn't we be happy that we are meditators?

- **Retreatant:** Didn't you say that this could never happen here?
- **Godwin:** Am I wrong?

❧ **Retreatant:** We never know.

❉ **Godwin:** We never know! That is a very interesting phrase to remember. This is a sentence a real meditator will always tell himself or herself. We really do not know what is going to happen. Can you say what emotions you will have in the next three minutes? Can you say what sensations you might have in ten minutes time?

This is a very, very important aspect in the Dhamma—to be open to uncertainty. Otherwise we have created a very secure world where we enjoy a kind of false security, where everything is controlled and we know what is going to happen. But the real security is being open to insecurity, the real security is being open to uncertainty. So you see what a profound teaching is in the Dhamma and if you can really take this in you are open to any experience, whether internal or external. When we have a relationship do we know what will happen in two years, three years, six months even? What about death? Who knows? Here is really opening up, being open to the reality of what life is.

In a way, it is a very hard teaching and in a sense it is for mature people. Shouldn't we be happy that we are mature people, that in the next few days we will be really open to any uncertainty? Externally rain or no rain, no problem. Internally pain or no pain, no problem. Plusses and minuses coming and going, being open to it all. We will try to arrange that one day we go to have breakfast and there is no breakfast! How would you relate to that situation? Something similar happens many times in everyday life. Ajahn Chah, one of the teachers that I really respect, a teacher from Thailand, was asked: What do you teach? Do you teach samādhi, calm, tranquillity; or do you teach vipassanā, insight? With a very mischievous smile he said: "I teach frustration!" That is what he does with his monks, creating situations where something unexpected happens. And he tells them: Look at your mind, are you holding on to your suffering or can you let it go?

So the Dhamma is something very simple, very practical, very direct. The Buddha often said: "I teach suffering and the way out of suffering." Then in any situation where we are suffering we have to see what we are doing, how the suffering was caused, and then, can we let go or do we hold on to it? So it is a powerful teaching. Isn't meditation interesting? Isn't spiritual life challenging?

2
MEDITATION ON BREATHING

Today we are going to have a very serious discussion. We have to discuss our friend, the breath. A question we can explore together is why did the Buddha choose the breath as an object of meditation?

Retreatant: Because the breath is always there.

Godwin: This is a very important point: it is always there. Even when we are sleeping, it is there. And, as it is there always, this is why we should relate to it as a friend. Who is the friend who is with us always? Even when we are asleep our friend is there. So it is very important to make a connection with our friend. And then during the day, when we are awake, the friend is always prepared, ready to tell us just to be in the here and the now. Because the breath always happens now, in the present. So in any situation, any moments when we are daydreaming, fantasising, getting lost in the past or in the future, the friend is patiently waiting. Any time one wants to experience the present moment, the reality, it is there to help us. What a friend we have! Any time, all the time, first point. What else?

Retreatant: The breath serves as a mirror

Godwin: The breath is always a mirror, or to put it in another way, it always indicates to us our state of mind, our emotions. Can anyone give a practical example?

Retreatant: When we get angry the breath is quickened.

Godwin: Not only when there is anger, but also when there is fear and anxiety it indicates our state of mind to us. And when the mind is calm, when the mind is relaxed, what happens to the breath then? When we are meditating and when the mind becomes calm, actually sometimes we cannot even feel that we are still breathing. I know some meditators who come running to me, saying: I think I have stopped breathing! That is one of the many problems meditators have! So as you rightly said: the breath, our friend is very useful, very objective; he or she is never mistaken. Who is the friend who can be always objective? In that sense the breath is like a mirror, it just reflects your condition objectively, just as you are. Anything else?

Retreatant: It reminds us that we are connected with the universe.

Godwin: All living beings have to breathe. So, as you rightly said, it reminds us of the Buddhist idea of interconnectedness, interrelationship. What Thich Nhat Hanh calls interbeing can easily be realised by connecting with the breath. It is also related to the fact that we are breathing the same air. We cannot say that this is my air, which is separate from other peoples'. You see what a deep, interesting, profound implication this has. Anything else?

Retreatant: It is coming and going, and changing all the time.

Godwin: Absolutely right. It is changing all the time. Rising, falling, coming, going. If you can really observe it, it becomes very clear how from moment to moment it is changing. Anything else?

Retreatant: You can smile with the breath.

Godwin: I think Thich Nhat Hanh said this beautifully: Breath in, feel calm, breath out, smile. So again, we can use our friend to feel calm, we can use our friend to learn to smile. And sometimes a smile can be infectious. It can infect others, again making a connection with others. Any more discoveries?

Retreatant: The breath reminds us that we are alive.

Godwin: We can use the breath to remind ourselves that we are living, and living from moment to moment, if each breath can be seen as the first breath or the last breath. I mean you are then really living from moment to moment. And at the time of dying this is also the last breath. I read one Buddhist text, where it said that if you practise this meditation at the time of dying then death may come naturally to you. So it helps us when we are living, and it helps us when we are dying. And again, it is the friend who will be with us until the last moment. The only friend who will be there until the last breath. And it helps us to experience calm, to experience some peace. It helps us to die peacefully. Anything else?

Retreatant: The breath shows us that there is a polarity—the in-breath and the out-breath.

Godwin: You use the right word: polarity. It is not just one way, one has to have these two processes. And this polarity can be used in a very important way. One thing is that in meditation it can sometimes be very useful to find out whether there is a difference between the in-breath and the out-breath. If the in-breath is long, does the out-breath also become long? And another very interesting aspect is what happens between the in-breath and the out-breath? Please try to discover this tomorrow if you have not already discovered it.

In the Tibetan tradition they use the breath to develop compassion: you breathe in the suffering of the world, you breathe out compassion for other beings. And I have been using it for developing loving-kindness—we might try it sometime tomorrow. Breathing in friendliness to yourself; breathing out friendliness to others. Breathing in forgiving yourself; breathing out forgiving others. Please try this. Because if you can develop this association, if you can make such a connection, then the breath will always have an association with loving-kindness. So that is another very positive aspect of our friend: whenever you think of your friend, loving-kindness arises. You can use this loving-kindness for yourself, and you can use this loving-kindness for others. See how the polarity can again be used functionally.

☙ **Retreatant:** The breath shows our connection to the environment.

❁ **Godwin:** That is why I said earlier that it really connects us with inter-being, our inter-relationships are shown up.

☙ **Retreatant:** It is an experience of reality when you are breathing with awareness: to be alive, physical sensations, coolness, freshness...

❁ **Godwin:** That is why it helps us to experience some calm. Another thing is it is so non-selective: there is no Buddhist breathing, there is no Christian breathing, there is no Hindu breathing. And equally it is non-selective between females and males.

There are so many divisions in this world: religious divisions, racial divisions, gender divisions and so on. Here there is not such a division. The friend is always reminding us to let go of these divisions—that itself is a valuable teaching. The friend is saying: Give up all these concepts, identifications, that you have. I hope when I go back to Sri Lanka I can tell this to the Tamil and the Sinhalese people also. Please stop the war. There is no Buddhist breathing, no Sinhalese breathing, no Tamil breathing. I hope they will listen to me.

Breathing and Awareness

An important reason why the breath is used as a meditation object is that it helps us to develop awareness. The meditation that we did today is called in Pali *ānāpānasati*. It is awareness or mindfulness or attention in relation to the in-breath and the out-breath. A problem meditators have is that they try to exclude other things, they try to exclude sounds, for instance. When they hear sounds they become a problem. When they have thoughts they also hate the thoughts. Poor thoughts! If they experience any sensations in the body, they think this is a disturbance or a distraction in the meditation.

But it is very simple: the first emphasis must be on awareness. Just being aware of whatever is happening. This gives us a very interesting experience: you hear sounds, so you are aware of the sounds. Then see with the sounds what happens to you, because we can convert sounds into noise, which is then disturbing us. It can be a very deep realisation, that the problem arises because of the way we relate to things. When I talk about sounds I sometimes speak about an experience we have in Sri Lanka in the meditation centre at Nilambe. There is a bell to wake you up at 4:45 in the morning. You can just imagine what association the sound of the bell has! But it is the same sound which is heard to indicate lunch. No difference. Where is the problem? It's in the meaning, the association. So it is not the sound, what you hear, but how you relate to it that is important.

As I was saying, the breath helps us to develop awareness, and while sitting we discover this very important skill. Then in everyday life it is a matter of using that skill we discovered while sitting. So you see this meditation has an important application in everyday life.

Another glimpse or experience we can have with the help of our friend the breath is that the friend helps us to be in the present. You may have a further realisation that even the idea of the present is just a concept. Then you can have a glimpse of what is described in the Dhamma as the timeless experience where the past, present, and future do not exist. It shows that our little friend can show us some very deep and profound aspects.

Another similar experience is what is taught in the Dhamma as *anattā*: there is no 'I' or 'me'. Here again you can have a glimpse that there is only the in-breath and the out-breath—there is no I or me apart from the in-breath and out-breath.

Another aspect which I tried to present today was how, with the help of the breath, to learn non-doing. It is very interesting that we are so used to doing things, controlling, manipulating, interfering. Because of this strong conditioning we cannot leave the breath alone. Some meditators come and tell me that they are really controlling their breathing. It is sometimes not very easy to get them to let go of the control. But what the breath is teaching us is to leave it alone. And then that helps us to experience this non-doing, this doing nothing. Allowing the body to do what it likes. In Sri Lanka we are very good in that non-doing! I think in the West you need to learn some non-doing. It is certainly true that we are so busy now, we are so active, that we have no time to stop and reflect.

This is one of the greatest challenges human beings have in this modern age where there is such a lot of activity, where one has to be extremely busy otherwise you are left behind. And in this activity, in this being busy, how does one create some inner space? How can one create some inner stillness? That is a real challenge. Take the case of people who are doing a job. A picture came into my mind of people who are getting down from a train—how they are walking or running from the train—it is like a horde of ants. But someone has to do the jobs. So if you are doing a job you have to be like the ants. Otherwise you arrive too late at the office. In Sri Lanka there is a register people have to sign, and if you come too late there is a red mark. So you cannot do slow walking meditation from the train. The red mark will be there!

That is the challenge we have, how to function in such a society, how to do things quickly, and at the same time have this inner space, this inner friendliness. This is a real challenge we have. I will talk about this on the last day: When you go back, how to be like ants and still be a meditator.

Retreatant: Ants are busy but they take care of each other.

Godwin: There is a simple explanation for that. Ants know their boundaries, we do not know our boundaries!

* * *

Discussion

Retreatant: When we are meditating we may feel tired and sleepy. What should we do in that situation?

Godwin: Very good, practical question. One suggestion is, just open your eyes. Another is, it is emphasised in the Buddhist texts, to have your spine erect. If you can have your spine erect then you do not normally feel sleepy or drowsy. Another suggestion is, you are welcome to stand up. So you can try some of these things and see if they work.

❧ **Retreatant:** The first question is, in Chinese it is said that we have got only one mind and we cannot use one mind for two things at the same time. And during our daily life we have to attend work and most of the time we are very busy, so how can we deal with our work and make friends with our breathing at the same time?

And the second question is, you said earlier that breathing is our best friend and is with us all the time even when we are sleeping, so when we have dreams or when we are in deep sleep how can we take care of our breathing at that time?

❀ **Godwin:** I'll start with the last question. What is interesting about our friend is that there are times when we can ignore it. Because when we are dreaming and when we are sleeping, in order to think of our breath we have to have awareness and consciousness. If you are a very advanced meditator you can have some element of awareness while you are sleeping and dreaming. Otherwise where is the person who is having awareness when they are sleeping and dreaming? So my response is, this is a situation where you can just leave our friend alone and he or she would not mind it at all.

The first question was that in everyday life we have to do many different things. Now when we have to do different things, how can we do these different things and still take care of our friend? As I said, to think of your friend you have to stop your work. This is why I said when the traffic lights are red, when you are just doing nothing, just be conscious of your friend, rather than being impatient about the red light. When you are having a particular emotion and when you are bothered by that emotion, at that moment you will not be trying to do different things, so then just come back to the breath.

Now I would like to respond to the question: What might we try to do as meditators when we have to do many different things? Here, what happens is that when we have to do various things we might have the idea: I have to do many things but it is possible I might make a mistake. Sometimes this is what creates the tension. As I said yesterday, in cultures where the emphasis is on doing things perfectly, correctly, you always want to do everything perfectly. So I think in such situations, if you can just let go of this idea of perfection this can be helpful. This is one suggestion.

Another interesting point is that although we have to do different things, we can, as you rightly said, do only one thing at a time. So that if we can learn to be conscious of whatever we are doing in any particular situation, then one can develop what is called moment-to-moment awareness in relation to what has to be done.

Maybe one last suggestion which can be very helpful is that when you are working, when you have to do many different things, as I said earlier, what is important is to become conscious of your state of mind. Are you anxious, are you stressed, are you insecure, or are you relaxed? It is very important for those of you who are really interested in everyday practice to constantly check out your state of mind. Whether you are working or whether you are not working, try to develop this practice of constant watching, awareness of what is happening in your mind.

When you have to do different things, after becoming aware of these different things, just watch your state of mind. Is it reacting or is it responding? These are two very interesting words: *reacting, responding*. Responding is doing what is necessary without reacting. Reacting is getting anxious, getting fearful, getting stressed, tense and so on. As you are still human and as you're still practising, it is human that you will start to react in certain situations.

So if you are not able to be conscious at the time you are reacting, at least later on, when there is space, when there is clarity, when you have recovered from that emotion, can you look back and find out: why did I react? Why couldn't I have responded in that situation? Then as I said yesterday, we can learn from our mistakes, we can learn even from our reactions.

This kind of inquiry has to be done without giving yourself a minus. You do have to do this kind of inquiry in a very friendly, gentle, playful way. And then you can experiment with it, you say: "Now tomorrow let me go to work and see what happens. Will I react, will I respond? And with any reaction, how long will it last?" So you keep an open mind to see what is going to happen.

These are very interesting, beautiful aspects of meditation, to see it as experimenting, experimenting with yourself. So when you try an experiment you don't take up a position. Without taking up a position, you're just learning, finding out, exploring. We can experiment, explore, and learn from any situation.

Retreatant: When I am aware of myself being aware of the thoughts, then in that case I cannot concentrate on my meditation, so what can I do?

Godwin: This is another point we have to think about, this word concentration. Those who have been listening to me carefully will notice I have not used the word concentration at all, but rather than concentration, the words I use are awareness, mindfulness, just knowing. I purposely avoid the word concentration because this is what is creating the problem, this is what is creating the suffering.

What I would suggest is: if the mind is concentrated, just know that the mind is concentrated; and if the mind is not concentrated, just know the mind is not concentrated. Then what is the problem? It is very important when we sit for meditation not to have an expectation, an idea, a model of what should happen or what should not happen. In the Zen tradition there is a beautiful phrase for it, to have a beginner's mind, or a don't-know mind. Expectation is what creates suffering in our life. When we have expectations and when things do not correspond to our expectations we suffer in life, and this is how suffering is created in meditation too. It is very interesting. So when we meditate without having any expectations, we will just try to know what is happening from moment-to-moment.

And it is very important not to give plusses and minuses when we are meditating. Someone is expecting to concentrate and then when you think you are concentrated you give yourself a big plus and hold onto the concentration—that's how tension is created! And when the mind is not concentrated we give a big minus! So in meditation also we are rating ourselves, giving plusses, giving minuses, giving plusses, giving minuses. This is what we are doing in ordinary life, so at least in meditation please learn just to be open to whatever is happening.

3
DEVELOPING A SKILFUL APPROACH TO MEDITATION

In meditation, in all the techniques, there is an aspect which is very much emphasised, and that is awareness. All techniques converge on two points: awareness and having an equanimous mind, a mind that is detached, a mind that is not identifying with things, a mind in a steady state of peace and calm.

Now why is awareness so important? Because it is the opposite of being like a machine—with awareness we become conscious of our reactions and responses, we build up self-knowledge and understanding. In what is called concentration one learns to focus the mind on an object like the in- and out-breathing. Now when we focus like that there is an aspect of control in it and exclusion, thoughts are arising and we push them away.

How does one do concentration meditation without getting into conflict? The conflict arises if you take up the position that you should not have any other thoughts. So my whole emphasis when teaching mindfulness of breathing is on being aware of what is happening. Sometimes the way this meditation is presented one has the impression that one should be aware only of the breathing—which for most people is impossible. Instead when thoughts, sensations, sounds, and so on arise, I suggest one learns to be aware of them, without developing conflict.

Why are we doing concentration initially? Because we have to learn to have a mind that is still, to have some space in our minds, some calm. Otherwise, if we don't do this there is confusion, disorder, distraction. When we can be more and more with the breath we establish stability. That is the first step.

When we have achieved a stable mind, and when we are alert, then we open up and let anything arise—this is choiceless awareness, and this is how we allow things from the unconscious to arise. In this meditation we don't have an object, we allow any thought or emotion or sensation to arise, we are not afraid. We don't make judgements.

In meditation in the first stage we are trying to work with what is there, and we may have negative emotions, restlessness, anxiety, fear, guilt. Whilst learning to focus on an object, we at least learn how to push these emotions away, and when they are pushed away then the jhāna factors arise—there is joy, happiness, one-pointedness, awareness. Positive emotions arise in the place of negative ones.

In the second phase we learn to be aware of both positive and negative without distinction, and to reflect them as they arise, just as they are. Joy arises and we reflect it just as in a mirror—and without the feeling this is 'my' joy, or 'my' restlessness—that is freedom, that is the model presented in the Dhamma.

HAPPINESS AND GRATITUDE

I would like to offer some other suggestions about the practice today. The first suggestion I would like to offer is that every one of you should feel happy that you are able to come here. Today is a holiday and after working very hard you should really feel happy about yourself that you have decided to come here. Usually we feel bad about ourselves, but it is very important to feel good about ourselves. I would like to emphasize this point, just to feel good about yourself that you are able to come here for meditation.

The next suggestion is to try to feel grateful that you are able to come. I know there were some who wanted to come today but for different reasons they were unable to come. You should feel grateful that you were able to come and that you are here.

Another important aspect related to this is to be mindful, to be aware with loving-kindness, just knowing what is happening with friendliness. It can be like a mother who is just watching, observing her only child with friendliness. So let us learn today to watch, to observe, to find out, just to know what is happening in our mind and body like a mother watching her only child, with friendliness, with gentleness, with openness.

Related to mindfulness is another suggestion I would like to offer: let us learn to slow down today. I know in Hong Kong you have to move very fast because the speed of life here is very fast. Today we will make it a point to learn to relax and just do things very slowly; slowly and also in a very relaxed way.

SILENCE

Another suggestion I would like to offer is the practice of silence. I know it is very difficult for some people to be silent because it is a very strong habit that we have to speak. So today let us make an effort just to be silent with ourselves and you will see a connection between awareness, mindfulness, and silence. The more aware you are, the more silent you become and when you are silent, mindfulness will come naturally. You'll enjoy the space that silence creates in your mind.

Another aspect of silence is learning to be alone with ourselves. So today please try to be silent and just be alone with yourselves. We have become so dependent on external things. But today we will try just to be friendly with ourselves and see whether we can be in our own company and enjoy our own company: learning to be our best friend. It is very important to make this connection with ourselves where we see ourselves as the most precious friend we have.

Now a question arises: How can we be silent and still practise loving-kindness? Here I would like to suggest that we can still relate to other people, connect with other people, in silence, with loving-kindness. Normally we know only how to communicate with words. But during this retreat we can learn how to communicate with others in silence. One way of doing this is to learn to be aware of the people around you. Another way is to smile at the people around you. So these are ways of making a connection with other people. And then when you look around, when you observe people, you might see opportunities where you can give a helping hand in complete silence. I would like you to develop this quality of communicating with others without words, in silence, and see whether one can make a deeper connection non-verbally.

SELF-RELIANCE AND OPENNESS

It is very important in meditation to be self-reliant, to have our own tools. The Buddha emphasised self-effort is the best effort, and to be self-reliant. So another very important suggestion I would like to offer is that we will try to develop self-confidence today, to have the self-confidence that you can handle whatever is arising in your mind and body. In meditation this is very important, to have this self-confidence; just to know what is happening in the mind and the body, and then learning from them, being open to them.

So today we will try to be like children, trying to learn, making discoveries about what is happening in our mind and body. It is very important to have this childlike quality of learning, finding out, being curious about what is happening in our mind and body, which is something we take for granted.

Try to see meditation as a voyage of self-discovery, and if we can have this openness then we can learn from any experience we are having today. As I said, it can be pleasant, it can be unpleasant, but we are learning to ask the questions: What can I learn from this? What does it show to me? This kind of attitude to meditation is very important.

One last suggestion is: please do not have high expectations that you are going to achieve something very special. Meditation is nothing special. It's just being open to ordinary things. It's nothing extraordinary. Please remember that. Please realise that. This is something beautiful about meditation. So it is not results that we are going to achieve but the practice itself: *that* is the result. Knowing what is happening is the result, not what comes after. Please remember this. Maybe in this culture there is a lot of emphasis on being goal-oriented, on achieving results. But in meditation the result *is* the practice. This is what is very interesting about meditation. The result is just being open, knowing what is happening from moment-to-moment, experiencing every moment.

4
LOVING-KINDNESS MEDITATION

Today has been a day of loving-kindness and one of the meditators told me that people were smiling at each other. They even broke the silence and said something very kind to one of the other meditators—so I thought one day of loving-kindness is enough!

Now, why do I emphasise loving-kindness so much? It is based on a very simple model of what I consider as Buddhist meditation. It is something very simple, very practical, very direct. What we need to do, firstly, is to develop a lot of loving-kindness. Loving-kindness to oneself, and loving-kindness to others. And if we can really do that, then we experience a lot of joy, a lot of bliss, a beautiful lightness both in the mind and the body.

And then, when you experience that, the moral aspect, the ethical aspect, is looked after by itself. Because if we have loving-kindness, if we have compassion, it is not possible to harm oneself or to harm others. It is not possible to be destructive to oneself or to be destructive to others. Then a kind of natural morality or natural ethical behaviour arises. There is a beautiful phrase in this connection in the Dhamma. The two Pali words are *anavajja sukha*, which means the bliss that comes from harmlessness. So that you never harm yourself nor will you harm others and that can really bring a lot of bliss, a lot of joy. This is the first step—and I must say—a very important step.

After that, if you want to go deeper, then you can realise that even loving-kindness is *anicca*, is changing, and that loving-kindness does not belong to anyone. There is no I or me that is practising loving-kindness, and you experience emptiness. This is my simple model of what I consider Buddhist meditation. And I feel that every human being who is motivated in this way is capable of achieving it. Only the other day I was thinking that we all have the necessary qualities of freedom and enlightenment. But these qualities are covered up, or as it is said in the Dhamma, they are obscured. But with more and more loving-kindness these qualities arise.

LOVING-KINDNESS FOR OURSELVES

I would like to say something very practical about how to develop the meditation of loving-kindness. It is interesting that we have to begin with ourselves because you cannot be friendly to others if you are not friendly to yourself. And when you begin with yourself where do you start? One has to start with the body. That is why in this retreat after Yoga I have been emphasising relating to the body. Over the years I have been meeting meditators who do not seem to like their bodies. Sometimes they even hate their bodies, and when one hates the body and when one dislikes the body, this can create many problems.

One problem is that it is possible that you can make your body sick in different ways. Because there is a kind of self-destructive aspect we have, and this self-destructive aspect can manifest itself in the body. It has been very interesting that when I travel in the West I hear there are even diseases in relation to eating food, what are called eating disorders. And I have been told this is mostly related to the way people relate to the body. In Sri Lanka the problem is that there is no food. And here because of food people become sick! This is very interesting for me. If I tell my friends in Sri Lanka about this they might not believe it.

Another way this dislike for our body can affect us is that we push it away, and do not look at some aspects of our body. So that this can result in feeling a kind of physical split, where part of the body is denied. I meet meditators who feel such a split in two ways. Sometimes it is a horizontal split, sometimes it is a vertical split. And I am sure this split is there psychologically also. They feel as if they are two different people.

Another thing I have discovered over the years is that people have tensions in the body, in different parts of the body. And these tensions that people carry are due again to the way they have been relating to emotions, the way they have been relating to their body. Therefore it is extremely important to begin the meditation of loving-kindness with our body. Really making friends with our body, really discovering our body, really learning to listen to our body. And learning to accept the body as it is, whatever you discover in the body. This is why I have been emphasising: please be open to unpleasant sensations, tensions, pleasures, whatever you discover in the body. This is briefly about the body.

Then we come to other aspects. One of these is—as I have been mentioning a lot—this idea of giving minuses to ourselves. In giving minuses to ourselves again we dislike ourselves, we hate ourselves. This can have many reasons, but I would like to mention one very important reason because this is related both to the physical splits and maybe also to self-destructiveness. As children we have been asked, we have been told in various ways, to be different from what we are. We have been given models, ideals, images of how we should be and naturally there is a split between what you are and what you should become. We begin with this and then people take it into their spiritual lives also. They come to what are called meditation retreats, and the meditation teacher says: You must be calm, you must have loving-kindness, you must have this or that, and so on. Naturally you cannot always achieve this. Then there is more self-hatred, more feeling yourself as worthless, as being a failure. So what to do with such types of meditation teachers?

This is why I now emphasise that as a first step—mind you, as a first step—to accept who you are honestly and very sincerely. To accept our humanness. To accept that we are still imperfect, because that is the fact, and to work from that fact, and to have loving-kindness towards what you are. This does not mean that you want to give in to what you are, but to work with these things with friendliness, with gentleness, with tenderness. So this is another aspect in developing loving-kindness.

Healing Mental Wounds

Another issue is what I call psychological wounds that are created maybe in childhood, or wounds that are created in subsequent relationships. It is interesting how these wounds are created in relationships. Now when there is a relationship, naturally you come to a conclusion, you have a model, of how the other person is. Usually you begin with a big plus. Otherwise how can a relationship begin? Very soon—after how long I do not know—slowly, slowly the minuses start coming. And this happens in a very interesting way: with the plusses we put the other person on a pedestal: "I have a wonderful girlfriend"; or "I have a wonderful boyfriend." And what happens after some time? They fall from the pedestal. It is natural that they fall, because you have put them on the pedestal. A big wound is created: I never thought he would behave in this way, I cannot accept it, I cannot believe it.

So the bigger the pedestal the bigger the wound. And then what do you carry as a wound? Hatred, ill-will, disappointment, frustration, hopelessness—we hold on to it all. Then we do something similar with ourselves. Especially when we turn to meditation and spiritual life, we put ourselves on a pedestal, thinking: I am practising loving-kindness now; I am sure I will not get angry now. And then you want to overcome craving. In fact I met a meditator today who says that he wants to completely overcome his craving. So then what happens? You fall from this high pedestal that you have placed yourself on. And the wound that is created is guilt. I meet many, many meditators who suffer very much from guilt. For some reason guilt is a big issue here. And this can be extremely self-destructive. Because with guilt you are really beating yourself. And you can also, with guilt, punish yourself. And you can punish yourself in different ways, in very subtle ways.

And when you have these wounds, what are their effects? One thing is that they can affect relationships. Without your knowledge, you can be creating suffering for yourself and suffering for others and the reason for this is not clear to you. And I have said how these wounds can also affect the body in two ways. They can cause what is called psychosomatic illnesses, and also they can cause certain blocks in the body: tensions, pains, and so on. And they can affect how we sleep—these things can come up in our sleep. Don't we start crying in our sleep? Don't we feel sad in our sleep? And sometimes without any reason you can have an emotion: you feel like crying, you feel sad, you have panic but you cannot find any apparent reason for it.

And what is more important is that at the time of death these wounds can come up. While living we can push them away, we can deny them, we can pretend that they are not there. But at the time of death they surface in a very strong way. Can anyone suggest a reason why this should happen at the time of dying?

༄ **Retreatant:** Because we are too weak to push them away.

❈ **Godwin:** Exactly. Because at this time we are mentally weak, physically weak. We can no longer push them away, and they can surface in a very strong way. So unless you heal these wounds you cannot live peacefully, you cannot sleep peacefully, you cannot die peacefully. Do you realise the importance of healing these wounds?

So how does meditation helps us to heal these wounds? I will offer some suggestions how they can be healed. The first suggestion is to find out how these wounds have been created in the first place. And when you find out the reason for that, you realise—as I said earlier—it is related to your own expectations, your models and so on. The second suggestion is to realise that holding on to these wounds can be extremely self-destructive. Another way is—as I have been suggesting—learning to forgive oneself and to forgive others. As I often say: to realise that you have been human and that the other persons have also been human.

Another way to work with these wounds is to understand how they arise. When we observe our thoughts and our emotions we realise that these wounds surface in relation to our memory. So, as they are in our memory, is it possible to completely erase them? Is it possible just to forget them? You will experience that the more you try to forget, the more you will remember them.

The more you try to push them away, the more powerful they become. And then what to do?

This is what can be done in a practical way. In unexpected situations these things arise in the memory, they are brought up, you remember them. As meditators we cannot prevent this from happening. But what we can do as meditators is to observe this process. The memory of the wound comes—anger. The memory of what we have done comes—guilt.

So one thing we can do as meditators is just to observe, just to see what is happening. And, if these emotions are arising, learn just to be with them—as I have been saying so often, creating space around them, making friends with them and saying: It is okay not to feel okay. This is meditation of loving-kindness.

Another thing which can be attempted is to sometimes deliberately and consciously bring up these wounds, these memories, because that is a way of making friends with them. Then, when they come up unexpectedly, the power and the energy that we have given to them may become less. Then when you continuously practice like this, one day you might have an experience where the memory comes and no reaction to it arises. That is an indication that the wound is healing. So these are some ways and means of healing these wounds. And the most important thing, which maybe is not so easy sometimes, is to realise that these things have happened in the past, and to learn to let go of the past. We cannot change the past, it has gone. And only when your wounds are healed can you really experience some peace again, some joy, and some lightness.

Another aspect of loving-kindness is using loving-kindness to work with our emotions, using loving-kindness to help us to work with unpleasant physical sensations and unpleasant states of mind. This can be a very powerful tool.

A further important aspect of the meditation of loving-kindness is learning to see more and more your plusses, more and more your positive qualities. When you see more and more of your positive qualities, you are bound to see more and more the positive qualities of others. This can again generate a lot of joy, a lot of happiness, to see these positive qualities in ourselves, and the positive qualities in others. And then you will be in a position to handle the minuses in you and the minuses in others in an entirely different way, with loving-kindness, with understanding, with compassion.

Gratitude

Another very important quality of loving-kindness is developing gratitude, feeling grateful. When I was in Bodh Gaya I heard this story of the Buddha, and I read it many times, that the Buddha, according to the story, spent seven days showing his gratitude to the tree which gave him shelter while he was struggling for enlightenment. When I reflected on this, it really touched me very deeply. Feeling grateful to a tree? Spending seven days there for the sake of a tree?

And if we reflect on our lives do we fail to show gratitude for what we receive from others? Do we express our gratitude either in words or with our expression when we get help from others? If a person can develop this gratitude towards a tree, how much gratitude should we have for people around us?

Do we feel grateful for the things that we are using? Do we feel grateful for some of the things that we take for granted? Do we feel grateful that we can see? There are people who cannot see. Shouldn't we feel grateful that we can hear the birds? There are people who cannot hear at all, who cannot hear the birds. As I said this morning, shouldn't we feel grateful and happy that we are discovering the Dhamma and we are making a commitment to practice the Dhamma?

Shouldn't we feel grateful for that? These are little things we take for granted, but these little things go a long way. So please realise meditation is not having special experiences, special qualities, extraordinary things. It is seeing these simple things, it is seeing these ordinary things—this is something truly extraordinary.

5
Sharing Our Experiences of Meditation

For the discussion, what we may try to do is to share each other's experience of what happened today. I feel it is very important to learn to share our experiences very honestly with a group of spiritual friends. Sharing both what we consider to be pleasant experiences and also unpleasant experiences. This is opening ourselves up to our spiritual friends. Normally we are very nervous, self-conscious, when speaking about ourselves, thinking that others will judge us—whether we have done the right thing and so on. You should not have fear about it because you are simply sharing your experiences.

So what is your experience with meditation? We started at 5 o'clock, are there any questions, any problems, any difficulties about the simple meditation that we practised: just knowing what is happening?

Retreatant: I was half-awake in this morning's meditation. I just went through it in a hazy way. But for reasons unknown, in the meditation just before this discussion I discovered something: I felt it was different from how I felt this morning. Before, it was like wasting a lot of my energy. I felt exhausted in having to be aware of our body movements and mental activity. It was like waiting for them to appear but they just never appeared. In the session of sitting we have just had, when I felt stillness, then I knew how to use what our teacher told us, how to be aware of how my body works, and knowing it very clearly.

Godwin: Thank you for sharing that experience. It is nice to hear of your unpleasant experiences in the morning and what can be considered as a pleasant experience in the evening. If you did not have the unpleasant experience, you wouldn't have made this discovery about the pleasant experience in the evening. So it shows that we can learn from unpleasant experiences, we can learn from pleasant experiences. Therefore we should learn to be open to both unpleasant experiences and pleasant experiences. Would anyone else like to share his or her experience of this morning's meditation?

SLEEPINESS

Retreatant: When we meditate at home, is it better that we don't choose a time when we are too tired to do meditation? This morning I was too sleepy. I was not strong enough to concentrate.

Godwin: Whether you are at home or here, I would like to suggest that you try to experiment with meditation when you are tired as well, otherwise it is very easy to say: I feel tired, I know my meditation won't work, so let me sleep. That's how we pamper ourselves. Always saying Yes to what the body is wanting.

We need to break that conditioning in a very friendly, gentle, kind way. It means some days to say Yes to the body and some days to say No to the body. So tomorrow morning if you still feel tired you must tell the body: "Yesterday I gave in to you, I said Yes, today, I'm going to say No". It is very important to learn to have this kind of dialogue with the body, with oneself. Sometimes learning to say No, and then you come to the hall, you come to meditate and you see what happens.

There is a very interesting dialogue in the Buddhist texts between the Buddha and a monk who was feeling lazy, drowsy, tired when meditating. The Buddha offered some very interesting suggestions on how to work with that condition. The first suggestion the Buddha offered was: change your posture. So if you are sitting, do some standing meditation, do some walking meditation. And I would like to suggest in that situation to do some fast walking, or to walk backwards, because to walk backwards you have to be very alert and awake. Immediately you start walking backwards you will be awake.

This reminds me of a meditation master in Thailand. He gave this suggestion to meditators: in that centre there was a well, a deep well, and he told his meditators to sit on the edge of the well. So if they were tired and fell in, they would die! Unfortunately there are no wells here!

Another suggestion the Buddha offered, if that did not work, was to rub your earlobes. I would see that as trying to stimulate the body. The Buddha said if that does not work, go out and look at the stars. Maybe the discussion took place in the evening like this when there are stars. I would suggest that as a way of trying to stimulate the mind by something external. If that does not work, try to think of something very inspiring from the Dhamma that will really develop a sense of urgency.

If that does not work, please induce the image of a bright light. Some meditators see a bright light, and maybe this monk was able to see such a bright light. So the Buddha said induce a bright light, and again it could stimulate his mind. And if that doesn't work, the Buddha said, then go to sleep! Why did he say go to sleep? Why was the Buddha encouraging that monk to sleep?

Retreatant: Is it because the body, when it gets tired, needs to take a rest?

Godwin: Yes, in a way. This technique, this experimentation, will help him to find out whether the tiredness has a psychological reason or a physical reason. So it shows that sometimes—and maybe most of the time—feeling tired is not something physical but it is psychological. With these different techniques the Buddha was encouraging this monk to find out whether it has a physical reason or a psychological reason. Then if the techniques fail it shows that the tiredness has a physical reason; then we should learn to feel kind to the body.

Awakening the Senses

It is also very interesting that the Buddha encouraged monks and meditators to experiment, to explore, find out for themselves. This is what I am encouraging you to do by observing, by learning to make your own discoveries about your mind and body and how they work. Our mind and body are so close to us, but in a way they are so far away from us because we have not learned, we have not discovered about them, we have not experimented. This is why in meditation one should see the practice as not for achieving certain states of mind but rather for learning, discovering, exploring. It is a beautiful way to relate to meditation.

So after the morning meditation we had tea from 6:00 to 6:30, and I suggested you go out and see things very sharply, see things very clearly. Would anyone like to share some experience in this regard?

Retreatant: At that time I tried to put your directions into practice by looking at things sharply and clearly, but no matter how hard I tried everything looked the same to me as usual. No sharper, no clearer.

Godwin: So you should try again tomorrow also. I'll say what I have in mind about seeing things very clearly. Suppose we are looking at a tree. Can we have our complete and full attention on seeing the tree at that moment? And is it possible to see the tree as if for the first time? This is really a very interesting aspect.

Is it possible to see things with less thought or no thought? Because when we see things with our preconceptions, we don't really see anything very clearly. This means really learning to awaken our senses. We have not made an effort to cultivate this awakening of our senses, the sense of hearing, the sense of seeing, so we have to make a conscious effort sometimes.

I think another aspect we have neglected is the sense of smell. So tomorrow let us all make an effort to awaken our senses, seeing very clearly, hearing things, and also smelling very clearly. There are some white flowers here and these flowers give off a very beautiful scent. So slowly, slowly, let us make an effort, let us experiment with it, let us play with it, developing our senses in this way. You can also try with the Buddha image here, just looking at the Buddha image with your complete and full attention, with less thought or no thought.

SILENCE AND SPEECH

Now about silence, how are you relating to silence? Is it disturbing you, is it okay? Any thoughts about silence? Any experiences about silence?

❧ **Retreatant:** It is difficult.

❀ **Godwin:** The fact that it is difficult shows it is a very strong habit that we have to talk. And you know it is very difficult to stop a strong habit. Some meditators told me that when they stop talking to others they start talking to themselves. And one meditator told me that when other people were silent she felt they were punishing her! So I think although it is difficult we should still experiment with such situations, and then ideally you realise how space is created by silence.

I think another aspect of talking is, perhaps, to prevent certain things from arising, things you have pushed away, repressed, controlled. In some very intense silent retreats some meditators tell me how, with the silence, they suddenly have memories arising from their childhood which had been completely forgotten. And sometimes some of these memories that come up can be extremely helpful for us to understand our behaviour.

Just to give an example of an experience one woman had: I would like to share that experience with you. She was in a 10-day retreat when suddenly she remembered that as a 7-year-old girl, she had tried to commit suicide by shooting herself in a dark room. She had completely forgotten this experience, maybe because it was very unpleasant for her. But it was a very helpful memory for her because she was still afraid of the dark.

Another thing was that she was very self-destructive. She would take risks with her body, and so on. Then I had a discussion with her and we realised that the suicidal tendency in trying to destroy herself was manifesting itself in different ways.

Another aspect of talking and silence is that when we talk we feel as if we are somebody. When we are silent we feel as if we are nobody, and we feel uncomfortable with this feeling of being nobody. Another important aspect of silence is that it helps us to be alone with our mind and body for some time. So silence has some very important and interesting aspects. I certainly agree that it is difficult but certainly it is worthwhile.

There is an interesting story from the Tibetan tradition about a retreat place where one has to practise complete silence for a year, and after one year the student can go and speak to the Master but can only say two words. After one year a student went to the Master and said: "More food!" Probably for the whole year he had been thinking only of food! Anyway, these are some thoughts about silence. I would like to suggest that tomorrow there will be times when you have to speak, and when you have to speak you should learn to speak with awareness, what is called *right speech*. So silence is important, right speech is important.

There are so many things we can learn from our speech. When we speak to another person, do we really listen to that other person? Can you speak clearly? Can you speak very briefly what you have to say rather than continuing to speak and sometimes confusing yourself and confusing others? How far can we be aware and mindful when we speak? We can learn these skills here.

In everyday life this is one of the greatest problems we have, the way we cause problems because of our speech, especially in relationships: how we can hurt each other with wrong speech. So, as I said, silence is important as it has many important aspects, and also right speech is important because that also has many aspects. The Buddha encouraged us to speak gentle words, kind words, helpful words, words which can be healing to others. On the other hand we can hurt another person with our words, they can be more harmful, they can hurt another person, more than something physical.

6
OBSERVING OUR THOUGHTS

Why are thoughts so important in meditation? Can anyone suggest a reason?

- **Retreatant:** Because they are connected to emotions.
- **Godwin:** Any other reasons?
- **Retreatant:** Because they are almost always there.
- **Godwin:** Exactly. From the time we wake up to the time we go to sleep thought continues. So one reason is because there is this continuity of thoughts. And even when we go to sleep the dreams we have can be seen as a continuation of our thoughts. This is what happens in everyday life. And what happens to you when you are meditating? Is there any difference?
- **Retreatant:** Sometimes I succeed to be in the present moment, then the emotions come up.
- **Godwin:** In other words, in everyday life we are unable to live in the present, but here we have moments where we can be in the present—that is the only difference. So you see how important it is to learn about thoughts, to make discoveries about them, because they are there most of the time.

  Now one interesting discovery meditators make is that when they try to focus on breathing thoughts still come. When you are listening to me now the same thing is happening. The thoughts you are having now, do you want them to come? What does it show about our thoughts?
- **Retreatant:** They just come when they want.
- **Godwin:** They are just coming. They are just coming mechanically, habitually, repetitively throughout the day,

whether you are meditating or not meditating there is no difference. This is something very interesting, very important to discover, that they just arise mechanically, habitually, and then what do we do? Do we allow them to just come and go?

᭾ **Retreatant:** Mostly we react in some way.

❀ **Godwin:** Very, very important word—we *react* to the thoughts in some way. And this reaction is mostly, as we have been saying, giving plusses and minuses to the thoughts. This is a very important experience for you, to realise what is happening when thoughts are coming and going. And this process of reacting is how thoughts are related to emotions. So one thing we might try to do is to see how far we can allow them to come and allow them to go on their way, learning not to react to them. And if you can do that, there is no need to stop thoughts, no need to get rid of thoughts, no need to get angry with thoughts. Then you come to an experience where, whether there are thoughts or whether there are no thoughts makes, no difference because the mind is not reacting.

CREATING STORIES

Another interesting thing we do with these reactions is that we create stories; perhaps constructing stories, manufacturing stories, creating stories from what has happened in the past, or what is going to happen in the future, or even sometimes from hearing things, seeing things, in the present. Constructing, constructing.

And we are very creative, very creative indeed. Sometimes we can be very creative in a destructive way with our thoughts. So it is very important to know when we are using thoughts destructively, which we will be going into now, and how to use thoughts creatively. Can someone give an example of a story that we create?

᭾ **Retreatant:** I just sit there and eat and somebody sits down near to me and makes a loud noise whilst eating, and there is the possibility I just hear, you know, or there is the possibility that I develop an aversion against him.

❧ **Godwin:** Yes, we can create a story out of that. Someone is sitting next to us and the person is making a very unpleasant noise. Why is this person sitting next to me? And why is she making this noise? I have been eating now for 20 minutes, but she is continuing to make the same noise. I think she is doing this to agitate me!

We are laughing. But this is exactly what we do—a very good example, I can go on and on. Earlier we spoke of some of our emotions as being like "monsters". And in these stories you see how many monsters can come at the same time? With just this person sitting there we can have many monsters coming. We can have anger, and because of anger we can have guilt, and because of anger and guilt we can be confused, and because we are confused—what is another emotion that can arise? Then you look around and see other people are sitting so calmly, and you feel jealous. You see how from this little sound, from this very little sound, within a few minutes four or five monsters can come. Aren't we funny? You see how we can be destructive with our thought.

Now you see how important awareness is, you see how important observing thoughts are. And in everyday life this is how we are creating our own suffering. The stories that we create become so real. If you can see a story as a story, then of course, there will be less arising of suffering or emotions, but when you take the story as something real, when you give reality and power to it, that is how emotions can come, that's how suffering can arise.

You see the implications of some of the meditation techniques, like focusing on breathing—where we are taught to be just in the reality of the present moment—and then to understand and see through the constructions that we make from our thoughts. Then we can have an understanding, a realisation, or distinguishing, of what is real and what we are constructing—what is *un*real.

I think in everyday life this is the real challenge we have. I'll be speaking more about it on the last day, because we realise that in a sense there is no difference between what is happening here, and what is happening in everyday life in relation to thoughts. So in everyday life I feel that what we can work with—more than states of calm and clarity—what we can explore, what we can investigate, is this very interesting and important area of thoughts and emotions: how they interact, and how we use them to construct stories. And then, how we become victims of the things we have constructed ourselves. This is one very important insight, discovery, exploration we can do in relation to thoughts.

Another important discovery we can make is how to work with the thoughts we are having and our states of mind. I would like to suggest that what can be more useful, more meaningful in meditation is not so much to be concerned about the thoughts, but to work with our state of mind in relation to the thoughts that are coming and going.

In this connection there is a beautiful metaphor that is used in Tibetan Buddhism which I like very much. It is where the mind is compared to the spacious sky and thoughts are compared to clouds: that is very beautiful. So that in practical terms, you allow thoughts to come and go like the clouds and then you remain in a non-reactive state with this spaciousness.

And as we are still human, it is nice to be human with some of the clouds, with some of the thoughts, and I am sure we will be reacting to some of them. And then, when there is a reaction, this is where we can use thoughts creatively, so then you explore and investigate the reactions.

Making Judgements

These reactions are generally related to this very strong habit we have of making judgements, of giving plusses and minuses. We need to learn about the judgements we make, and sometimes we need to use judgements functionally. But this simple way of putting it, understanding our plusses and minuses, I feel opens up a very, very important area where we can explore how we are relating to ourselves and how we are relating to others with this process of giving plusses and giving minuses. Again, what is interesting is that we never question our plusses and minuses! From where have they come? Who taught us to be our own teachers, giving ourselves marks and so on?

Retreatant: We ourselves, because we behave like we think we have to, or how we ought to behave.

Godwin: So we have first of all got it from society, we have got it from others.

Retreatant: Or from meditation.

Godwin: From meditation, very good—I will speak about that. And here again, what we are doing most of the time is to use the plusses and minuses in a destructive way. It is a real test we have, a real challenge we have, how to use thoughts creatively, how to use thoughts functionally, and to see the difference when we are using them in a very destructive way, creating suffering for oneself and creating suffering for others.

Let's take how meditators in a meditation retreat use plusses and minuses in the context of meditation. You have one sitting where your mind is calm, is very clear, is very peaceful, and you come to the conclusion: At last it is working! Maybe I should now go deeper in meditation, maybe I should go to Sri Lanka or Burma, and deepen my practice and enhance my practice, and so on, and so on.

Now at the next sitting after lunch, you're feeling sleepy, feeling drowsy, there's no calm, the person next to you is moving around, maybe he has a cold, or whatever. You give yourself a big, big minus, thinking: During the morning sitting I had a pleasant experience, but I know in the long run these things don't work for me. I have never succeeded in life! So you can feel worthless, you can feel hopeless, you can feel useless, and then you compare yourself with others. One identity arises in the morning, another identity in the afternoon. This is what happens to meditators in retreats.

So you see how important our thoughts are, you see how important our plusses and minuses are. Then I am sure we are doing the same thing in retreats when we judge others. This judging is first about ourselves, and then we do the same with others. How do we judge others in a meditation retreat? Do you have any experiences? Your likes, your dislikes, your plusses, your minuses, do you ever question them? And the danger is we think they are always correct! Especially when we are judging other people, but even when judging about ourselves, we are so certain, no question about it.

Making Discoveries about Thoughts

Take the example of our conclusions—is it easy to change our conclusions, our assumptions? We become so fixed with them. And if someone questions them, there's another reaction. This came to me very clearly on one occasion; I've just remembered it now. I go to a so-called psychiatric clinic once a week when I am in Sri Lanka. It's a big joke among my friends, they say: Godwin goes to a psychiatric clinic once a week, claiming to help the people there, but we don't know who is helping whom!

In one of these clinics I met a young man, very, very sharp, very intelligent, with a very clear mind, a law student. He told me that he has a problem in his spine. He said that his spine is not correct, not straight, and that people can see it, and when people see it they talk about it, they laugh at it, so it is really a big, serious problem for him. It really makes him sad and depressed. So he doesn't like to go out, he likes to stay in his room, and so on.

I realised that actually there was nothing wrong with his spine but it was mostly in his head, with his thoughts, with his thinking, with his beliefs, with his conclusions. And when I tried to tell him this, he dismissed it. Then it occurred to me to say: Alright, shall we take an X-ray? Yes, he said, why not? Very simple, so we arrange to take one. Then the X-ray came back and the spine was quite normal. He looks at it and he says: "Yes, but my problem did not show up on the X-ray!" And at that moment what I thought was more about me rather than about that person. I thought: "Who knows, some of the conclusions I have, some of the assumptions I have, some of the plusses and minuses that I give—all this can be just like this person. Who knows?"

So it was clear to me that we live in a private world of our own. We have constructed a private world from our experiences, from our plusses and minuses and so on, and we are living in that private world. And this private world does not correspond to reality. And again from this private world we project our plusses, our minuses, our judgements, and we gather more and more experiences into our private world.

This is why there is no communication between people. People living each in their private worlds, how can there be any communication? That day one of the retreatants said it very well: "We are wearing coloured glasses."

In meditation, what we are trying to do, at least in the first place, is to acknowledge this, understand this; then to see how our private world, our subjective world, how the world we have created functions, how it operates. So you see the importance of being aware. Do you see the importance of being alert and awake about how our minds operate? And then slowly, gently, tenderly, and—as I have been emphasising very much—from our own experience, learning to see things as they really are.

I'll be talking more about this meditation that we have been trying to do—where we allow thoughts, emotions, and sensations to arise and learn to see them just as they are, without a plus, without a minus and see the difference it makes to us.

Finding Out about Ourselves

Another discovery we can make about our thoughts which I suggested today is to find out what really happens when there is a thought. What is our experience when there is thinking?

❧ **Retreatant:** Sometimes I have the feeling that at the basis of one thought or all different thoughts there is a feeling, and this feeling has been repressed very often in our lives, and this is connected with our old wounds. And then this repressed feeling is an energy source for new thoughts.

❈ **Godwin:** So we recycle thoughts. Recycling is okay when it refers to waste and so on, but recycling thoughts is not okay, because for every cycle, the emotion gets bigger. Anything else?

❧ **Retreatant:** I think anxiety and sorrow are reasons for thoughts.

❈ **Godwin:** I am a very simple man. I will give a few simple examples for you to realise what happens in our minds when there are thoughts. Let us think about the dinner we had. What happens to your mind when you are thinking about dinner?

❧ **Retreatant:** I see an image.

❈ **Godwin:** Exactly, we see pictures. If I close my eyes and think of the dinner I see pictures of bread, I see pieces of cheese, I see some tea. So our thoughts are mostly pictures. If you want to be clearer, use simple examples. You can think of breakfast. Now what are you seeing, what is happening in your thinking of breakfast?

❧ **Retreatant:** Like a commercial, I see a big cup of coffee.

❈ **Godwin:** I would like you to make more such discoveries. There are some very interesting exercises to do. This is what I am encouraging you to do, to make your own discoveries. Forget what you have read, forget what you have heard. Just be simple and practical and find out. This can be so fascinating, if you can have the openness to learn, you can discover so much.

This is meditation. Not taking anything for granted. I mean, how fortunate we are, how grateful we should be that we have this fascinating experience. I call it the laboratory of mind and body. But it seems that though this mind and body are so close to us, they are in many ways so very far away. So please, generate a fascination for this, please find a taste for this, please develop a curiosity for this. Find this the most meaningful thing you can do in this life, to discover what is so close to us. Feel happy about this, feel grateful about this, and feel enthusiastic about this.

Because it is fascinating, it is learning all the time about thoughts, about emotions, about perception, about so many things in this world of ours.

It is really a blessing that we have this fascinating mind—sometimes very complicated, very subtle, but always interesting, fascinating. The only thing is, you need to be very simple. This is very difficult. We are good at complicating very simple things. We had this when we were children, we were curious, always asking questions, but we have lost this curiosity. It is so beautiful, when you talk with children, how clearly they speak, because they just speak from their heart, from their experience.

I'll just share two experiences of mine in this connection. One was with a child who was about five or six years old, this was in Switzerland, I think, and she was telling me about swimming. I cannot swim, so I asked her: Can you teach me to swim? She said: It is very simple: lie on the water with courage. If I had asked a professor of swimming, he or she would have given me a one-hour lecture and I'd still be confused about what swimming is. This is the beauty of childlike simplicity. They speak from their heart, from their experience. By the way, then I asked her: What to do if I don't have courage? Very innocently she said: Then you won't be able to swim! Simple, isn't it?

Another experience: it was at a retreat like the one here, but it was a weekend retreat and like the sweet child we have here there was a young girl and the mother said she had just come for one day and asked if her daughter could sit with us in meditation. So I said: It will be nice to have her with us. Then I gave this exercise of just listening to the sounds, and after that I had a discussion with them and asked: Now, what actually happened to you when you heard these sounds? There were about 25 to 30 people, so they all gave very lengthy, long-winded explanations. Some were confused by the exercise. Some were not giving details of what happened, they were asking questions from me. And then it came to this child. She used just one word: Floating. She was just floating with the sounds, just being with the sounds. Immediately I said: Please, let us have a discussion on how we have complicated our minds. Because it was such a touching, moving experience for everyone present when this little girl, who had never meditated before, used just one word, unlike all these other people.

You see what I am doing, I started by talking about thoughts, and slowly, slowly I'm going on to different topics! So now let me pause and I am sure you will have questions. Please ask questions, especially in relation to everyday life. I am much more concerned about what happens in everyday life rather than what happens here, especially in relation to working with thoughts.

* * *

Discussion

Retreatant: How can I be in the present moment, and also find solutions for my problems?

Godwin: I think when you are a child there are not a lot of problems, so it is easy to be in the present moment. But when you are grown up you have serious problems, you must look after your family and pay your bills, and so on. Then you are thinking: "How can I solve my problems? How can I be silent, how can I be in the present moment and still find solutions for my problems?"

It is a very useful question. It is interesting that when I said to observe your thoughts, I never spoke about being in the present moment. Because thoughts are always about the past and the future, so the question of the present doesn't arise. So in everyday life please forget about being in the present moment! What is important in everyday life is, as I said, that from morning till night there is a continuous flow of thoughts. Just find out, just learn about it. It has nothing to do with being in the present.

Being Gentle

Retreatant: I do not have a question but I would like to tell about an experience. I wanted to do my 'homework', so I wanted to examine where my ideas come from. I found it takes a long time for a thought to come. A thought only came when I stopped trying to examine the process.

Godwin: A very interesting experience. I would like to say something, because it brings out a very important principle. When we do not want thoughts to come, when we are focussing on breathing what happens? They come and come and come. And when we say, Now let any thought come, they do not come! Why is the mind functioning in opposition to us? When a child is disobedient we say he is obstinate. Why are our minds so very obstinate? That is a very important question to explore. The same thing with emotions—when we invite the monsters to come, they do not come.

I will offer a very simple explanation. This is connected with the reason why I have been saying: Make friends with the mind. You cannot tell the mind: "Do this, do not do that", like a child. Yet this is what we are doing here in meditation. We come here, we sit in an unusual position and tell the mind: "No thoughts, no sounds, no one should be moving, no one should cough". We want something different, something special from the mind. Then after meditation we go out and then our mind can do anything it wants! So this is what is called meditation. Coming here, sitting, the fighting, the battle, and afterwards we go out. This is why I say, after the bell is the best meditation! Because you are not doing anything special, you are just relaxed.

Oh, you have to be friendly, you have to be gentle, if you want to understand a child. By telling the child: "Do this, do that", you cannot understand the child. But if you want to understand the child, create space for her, just watch her in a friendly way, then you will understand—this is what the child likes, this is what the child does not like. In the same way, you should have this connection with your thoughts, this is why I have been so much emphasising this friendliness, this gentleness, just finding out. Thank you for sharing the experience. Any other questions?

Retreatant: I had a very similar experience once on a retreat: when I went for dinner, I was asked not to label food—of course, I did not succeed, and it reminded me of a short story. There is a Jewish businessman, he goes to his rabbi, and says: "I am pretty rich but I could be a little bit richer. I have heard you are able to make gold." The rabbi says: "Yes, I can." "Oh, can't you tell me how to make gold?" The rabbi says: "It is very easy, you need a big pot and you fill it with water and then you stir it on the fire for three hours and always think gold, gold, gold …" The man says: "Then after three hours I have gold? It sounds so easy." The rabbi says: "There is only one problem: you are not allowed to think of a green crocodile." The businessman goes home, takes a pot with water, stirs it on the fire. The first thing he thinks is, "I am not allowed to think of a green crocodile!" That is what happens to me when I try not to label.

❀ **Godwin:** There is a similar story from the Tibetan tradition. The teacher tells the student: "You know that to get rid of thoughts by trying is not possible." But the student disagreed with the teacher. Then the teacher said: "Alright, then go and do not think of monkeys." And you can imagine what happened. He was thinking of monkeys, not only thinking but he was also imagining monkeys, and eventually the time came when he imagined that the monkeys were chasing after him! Then he goes running to the teacher and says: "Please, save me from the monkeys!" See how a small thing, a story, a fantasy, can become so real.

Experiencing without Words

I would like to say a word about the exercise I gave, listening to sounds. It shows how strongly conditioned we are by words. When we hear sounds, we feel compelled to recognise and label the sounds. And then by recognising the sounds, we can create a big story. It is a very interesting exercise to experiment with, to explore, to see what happens if you can just listen to sounds without the words, without the past associations, just the sounds.

When we see things we have given each thing a label, too. It is a very, very strong habit that we have. Again experiment, just play with these things. Take away the word and see things without the word. See whether there is a difference.

We do the same thing in attaching words to emotions and sensations. One of the tools I offered yesterday in working with emotions was taking away the word and just being with what you are actually experiencing. Please explore this for yourself. It is extremely difficult because it is such a strong conditioning we have.

Retreatant: There are a lot of books about positive thinking. Whenever I try to do that, something negative comes up!

Godwin: It is the same process. We have been so conditioned that it has become a habit to give ourselves minuses, it is so strong in us. And then learning to work with this, and learning to give plusses—that's very, very difficult. This shows how strong our conditioning is. It shows how strong our addictions are. It shows how strong our habits really are. So meditation is really working with problems or habits or conditionings. To use computer language: to de-program oneself.

Retreatant: When one becomes enlightened then do we have no more thoughts?

Godwin: I think there is nothing wrong with thoughts. This is what I have been trying to impress on you. What I have been trying to impress on you is how we use thoughts destructively. This is what you have to see in everyday life: when we use thoughts destructively, that is creating suffering. I also said how one can use thoughts creatively. So thoughts have a really very positive use. I would suggest an enlightened person would have thoughts but such a person will not use thoughts destructively.

There is a very interesting quotation by the Buddha himself in relation to his own thoughts: I would like to relate the details. One of his disciples told the Buddha: You have so many powers, you have so many miraculous powers. And the Buddha said: My greatest miracle is that when a thought arises, I know a thought has arisen; when a thought continues, I know that a thought continues when the thought disappears, I know the thought disappears.

This shows it is not the absence of thought which is important. I like that very much. We can try to work on the third aspect: when a thought disappears. For someone to have that type of mind they have to have a very calm mind, an alert mind, just to know when a thought disappears. So that's about the thoughts of an enlightened person. I think we should not worry too much about enlightened people!

Retreatant: Today during the meditation I tried to put more effort into observing the thoughts, and I discovered that when I put more effort into observation there were fewer passing thoughts. It's just like you said, when you invite emotions they do not come, when you invite thoughts they do not come also. It's very interesting.

Godwin: It's a very important discovery. When we don't want thoughts to arise they arise, and when we want thoughts to arise they don't arise. When we don't want emotions they arise and when we want emotions they don't arise. Why is the mind acting in opposition to us? This is a very important question to reflect on. Is this the nature of the mind? Or have we conditioned the mind in this way?

I think what it shows is that we cannot tell the mind: "Have thoughts, have no thoughts." It doesn't work that way. It's like telling a child: "Do this, don't do that." And the child likes to do what you don't want him to do. This is why I emphasise friendliness such a lot. If you want to understand a child you have to be very friendly and see what the child wants. So in the same way if we want to understand our mind we cannot be telling the mind to do this and don't do that, but rather, with friendliness, try to understand it.

So when there's friendliness, when there's gentleness, when there's openness, then the mind may start co-operating with us. Otherwise we tell the mind to behave in one way and it is going the other way and we get angry about it. It then becomes a battle and becomes another big fight. Meditation for most people is a fight. Fighting the mind. I often tell meditators, you have enough battles in life, please do not make meditation another battle!

With friendliness we need to understand how our mind and body works, and then through that understanding, developing mastery is the next thing. When I spoke on loving-kindness I mentioned that one of the benefits is that when there is loving-kindness the mind becomes calm naturally.

THOUGHTS AND EMOTIONS

༄ **Retreatant:** My thoughts are formed by words. I do not know whether the thoughts of others are also formed by words.

❀ **Godwin:** It's a very interesting discovery you have made that thoughts are really words. Words and pictures, and they give rise to feelings. Let's take a couple of examples. Let us think of breakfast tomorrow. Let us close our eyes and see what happens to our mind when we think of breakfast tomorrow. We see bread, we see coffee, whatever is usually there, we see. Actually these are pictures that come, and then with the pictures some feelings will come depending on our likes and our dislikes. So actually our thoughts come in the form of images, words and feelings. It sounds so simple. And then what happens to us is that with these things, these pictures, films, we create our suffering.

What is interesting is that with techniques like focusing on breathing, when there are no thoughts none of these things like pictures and words are present, but we are just dealing with the sensations. Words and pictures are always from the past. We can never see pictures and images which we have not experienced before. Only when they are absent can something new happen. This is the beauty of some of the meditation techniques—that they help us to have no pictures and so on.

So this is what I have been encouraging you to do, to make your own discoveries about your thoughts, make your own discoveries about your emotions, make your own discoveries about how suffering is created. We are so fortunate to have this mind and body. Sometimes I tell meditators that we can be our own laboratories and we can make experiments, we can make discoveries, we can learn from them.

Without taking anything for granted our whole life becomes learning; and we should develop a taste for it, we should develop a curiosity for it, we should find this very interesting, entertaining, sometimes amusing. So then when you leave this place you can continue to discover, you can continue to learn, you can continue to find out. Then we have this openness that we can learn from anything, we can learn from anyone, not only from the so-called teachers, but life itself becomes the teacher, our mind and body become our teacher, and I think it is a beautiful way to live.

Yesterday we were talking about relationships. Just watching the dogs that come here reveals very interesting relationships. What have we learnt from just watching the three dogs that come here? Have you watched them? It is very interesting to see their relationships. Just like humans. Fascinating to watch.

Talking about dogs, I would like to share with you an experience I had on one of the retreats I gave in a foreign country. On the last day I was having a talk with the meditators and one of them told the group that whatever she has learnt from me on the course she has already learnt from her dog. So I became curious about her dog. I told her, please tell something more about your dog, and she said: Well, you tell us to just live in the present and this is what my dog does; you tell us to feel grateful, and my dog is always grateful. And she went on to describe the behaviour of the dog and what happens in the retreat. Then I asked her: Is there no difference between your dog and me? She said, Yes, you talk a lot, but my dog can't talk at all! I like that story very much.

7
MEDITATION PROBLEMS

What I would like to discuss with you is what actually happens when you are meditating. Just share your experience and ask questions in relation to your experience while you were meditating. So can I ask: are there any problems, any questions about sitting meditation? I said just sit and try to know what is happening in your mind and body. Are there any questions, any difficulties about this?

Retreatant: While I meditate I have lots of thoughts and some are so obvious you don't need to observe them, but some are delicate, minor ones. Is it necessary to observe these thoughts?

Godwin: We should try to observe every thought. When I gave instructions for the meditation, I said: Can you be conscious of every thought that arises in your mind? And it is very important to learn to observe thoughts without judging them: this is delicate, this is not delicate, this is good, this is bad. Without judging, without giving plusses and minuses, can we just observe the thoughts as they arise and as they pass away?

PROBLEMS WITH THOUGHTS

Retreatant: I was thinking about anxiety. I have had anxiety for some time, but when I try to call it up and look at it, it doesn't come—or not in such a strong form as I used to suffer from. That is the first thing. Another thing is that if someone has had anxiety over a problem and cannot recall the anxiety later, then when the problem crops up again there is no time to practise, to have enough experience to face the problem and examine the anxiety and to get rid of it and to face the problem squarely.

❦ **Godwin:** My answer to the first point is: Can there be a problem when you wanted anxiety to come and it didn't come? What's the problem? Isn't it interesting: when we have anxiety it's a problem; and even when we don't have anxiety it's a problem!

❧ **Retreatant:** I want to know if there is any *should be* or *should not be* when we meditate. For example, when I'm doing the sitting meditation I can't stop thinking. It seems that when I'm doing the walking meditation the situation is better, but when I'm sitting, when thinking comes up I have a conflict whether to stop it or just allow it.

❦ **Godwin:** I'm happy you have raised that question because it is a very common problem. It is not possible to stop thinking. The more we try to stop thinking the more thoughts we have. That is why when I gave the guided meditation I said it is natural that thoughts will arise. So, as in the first meditation we did, what we were trying to do is to be aware, to be mindful of the thoughts themselves: thoughts, sounds, sensations, whatever there is in the mind and the body. In that sort of meditation if you have thoughts there is no need to have a conflict.

Also in the second meditation we did in which we were trying to be aware of our breath, when thoughts come we should be aware, mindful, that thoughts are coming, and make friends with them—not to have a conflict—and then come back to the breath. But we can be aware of the breath for a few minutes, then again thoughts will come. This is the nature of the mind, that we don't have much control of it. So meditation helps us to understand how our minds work by making friends with our mind and whatever is happening, and training ourselves to slowly, gently come back to the breath.

It is very important, even when we are not sitting, to continue to be aware and mindful of the thoughts that we are having. Even while relaxing, while eating, we are having thoughts. So whatever we are doing it's a very good practice to be conscious of our thoughts, not only when we are meditating. We can learn a great deal about our thoughts by just watching them, just asking: What are the thoughts that I'm having?

Most thoughts are either about ourselves or about others. And sometimes the thoughts are negative about yourself, negative about others; the practice is just to know how we are having negative thoughts about ourselves and others and how, when we have such negative thoughts, emotions are created. These are very important insights to develop by watching thoughts. Do we have more thoughts about the past? Do we have more thoughts about the future? Why do I have more thoughts about the past? What happens when I think about the future? Do I have anxiety? This is why we have to find out, learn, about our thoughts and how the thoughts can create emotions and how they can create suffering. This is a very important aspect of the practice. So it is not only stopping thoughts but understanding, learning, discovering about them.

Physical Problems

Retreatant: I've been meditating for over a year and I have lots of problems like my body moving, my ankle hurts, and after meditating for a while when I try to get up I have difficulties, but after I walk for a while it is okay. Now my left shoulder hurts. So I'm having all these problems. I want to know if I'm doing the meditation in the right way.

Godwin: I don't see them as problems. I tried to make it very clear that meditation is just knowing whatever is happening in our mind and body without being concerned: Am I doing it right? Am I doing it wrong? Is it very strange that this should happen? I repeated a number of times: Just to know what is happening, and see if you can say OK to whatever is happening, especially if it is unpleasant.

Anyway I would like to repeat that it is extremely important to learn to work with unpleasant sensations in whatever forms they arise in the body just by knowing them and learning to make friends with them, and not to see them as problems. That is the practice, because while meditating if you learn to handle these unpleasant sensations that arise then in everyday life when they arise you know how to handle them. So it is very helpful that these unpleasant sensations arise when you are meditating.

ೀ **Retreatant:** During the meditation I found my back perspired a lot; I got all wet. The second question is, when I focus on breathing my breathing becomes very quick. When I try to focus on something else then my breathing returns to normal.

❈ **Godwin:** The first question about the perspiration in the back, just know that there is perspiration in the back and let it be there. Make friends with that perspiration. About the second question, that when you focus on breathing the breathing becomes fast and when you focus on something else the breathing becomes normal, I would suggest in the beginning allow the body to breathe naturally, forget about focusing on the breathing but just sit and let the body breathe the way it likes. So please spend some time just learning what is called non-doing, allowing the body to do what it likes in relation to breathing. Don't see it as meditation but just see it as some exercise that you are trying to develop, just non-doing, allowing the body to breathe the way it likes.

There is a meditation master in Sri Lanka who says that when we sit, if we think meditation is something special then we will have special problems! So here we are trying to give special attention to the breath, and then the breath behaves in an unusual way and when you ignore the breath it becomes normal. Don't see meditation and breathing as something special, just be with it. And even when you are outside, when you think you are not meditating, just continue to have a connection with the breath, to continue to be aware of the breath at other times also.

Unusual Experiences

ೀ **Retreatant:** I want to talk about a personal experience of mine. Once after I read a *sutta* I went to meditate for about ten minutes. What happened was that there were lights flashing in my eyes. It was a golden light. Whether I opened my eyes or closed my eyes the light still flashed for more than half an hour. So I was a bit scared of this phenomenon that arose. I did not know whether this phenomenon was normal or abnormal and I would like to know how to handle this phenomenon.

❈ **Godwin:** Seeing visions, seeing such things reflects different phases in the practice. Sometimes these visions, these pictures you see are very pleasant, sometimes they are very unpleasant. As I was saying very often today, whether it is pleasant or unpleasant just know that you are seeing lights, you are having this experience, without thinking: Is it abnormal? Is it normal? If you react in that way you are getting involved with what is happening. So what you need to do is not to get involved but just to know; and, as I was saying, just to say OK and then after some time the sensation of lights or whatever will stop.

Becoming Pre-occupied with Oneself

There can be a danger in meditation, especially when trying to develop awareness, where, without knowing it, one may become very preoccupied and concerned with oneself, and then have utter disregard for all the people around you. This may result in an individual becoming deeply introspective in an unhealthy way. So I suggest to people therefore two things: One is that I always try to encourage people to focus their attention on things outside of themselves, developing their relationship with nature, for instance. With that focus one can then develop a good balance between intro- and extra-spection.

The second thing is that I encourage people to relate to the people around them, to build up sensitivity and concern, to care for one another, to have compassion for one another, and to relate together as spiritual friends. In this way one learns, in a meditation situation, how to relate to people around you, rather than to escape from them or simply avoid them. Withdrawing from people sometimes stems from the fact that people can hurt you, so rather than working with that situation, one finds that the easy thing to do is to escape from it. There is an instance in a Buddhist text where a particular monk wanted to live in seclusion but the Buddha advised him against it, but still he insisted and so eventually off he went. His retreat wasn't very successful, and he returned to the Buddha who then recommended five guidelines, one of which is to have spiritual friends around you.

Concentration by itself can be a form of self-security. It can also strengthen the ego. This is why in the Dhamma choiceless awareness is always related to compassion. There is a beautiful phrase that is used: boundless compassion—it means having no religious boundaries, no racial boundaries, and so on. Then your sense of separateness disappears, and you have a feeling of oneness where there is real compassion and no differences between oneself and the other.

8
A MIND LIKE A MIRROR

This morning I thought Sri Lankan weather had come back! I threw away the coat I was wearing and I was embracing the weather. I wanted to go for a walk, but I was expecting a meditator. Still, I could enjoy the morning from my room. Then in the afternoon, most unexpectedly there was rain, the sky became cloudy. In the silence, German weather has come.

How does one relate this to our practice? When the Sri Lankan weather is there, can we learn to see the beauty in the Sri Lankan weather? Can we be open to the Sri Lankan weather? And then, can we do the same with the German weather? Can we see some beauty in the German weather as well? One can see beauty in the mist. One could listen to the sound of the raindrops. In the late afternoon sitting there was a beautiful stillness, even the birds were not singing, a complete stillness in the trees.

Being one with the German weather as well, being open to the German weather as well. No plus for the Sri Lankan weather, no minus for the German weather. They are there due to certain conditions and due to certain conditions they are passing away. So our practice is really awakening ourselves to this duality, to be one with the Sri Lankan weather, to be one with the German weather. As Thich Nhat Hanh says: Feeling one with your sadness, feeling one with your joy—learning from joy, learning from sadness.

EXPERIENCING WITHOUT JUDGEMENT

To see these things, to awaken our mind to them, that is why we are getting up in the morning and doing yoga, practising silence, sitting for long hours with pain, having individual and outdoor meditation, listening to discussions: all these are tools to develop such an understanding, to awaken our mind to that state or condition. Is it not a very simple, practical model? Are we clear about our practice now? So the real challenge is whether we can do the same in relation to what is happening within us as we do to what is happening outside us. In relation to what is happening within us, how can we be open and awaken? As I have been saying so often: By learning to see things as they are. Whether the monsters are there or whether the monsters are not there, to learn from both conditions.

Now to describe this practice, this perspective, there is a very useful metaphor that is used in spiritual traditions and it is called having a mirror-like mind. Let us try to understand in practical terms from our own experience what it is to have a mirror-like mind. In what way can we practice to have a mirror-like mind? I have come across this metaphor in the Theravada tradition, in the Zen tradition, in the Tibetan tradition, and in Taoism as well.

Now in the Buddhist tradition there are two aspects to meditation: one is called calm, tranquillity, and the other is vipassanā or developing insight and wisdom. In developing calm and tranquillity I would say that this is like polishing the dust off the mirror. This is what we do, maybe, by practising with an object like breathing, where with the help of our friend the breath we learn to develop some calm, some tranquillity, some space, clarity and awareness. And when the dust is not there the mirror reflect things just as they are.

Being Open to the Pleasant and the Unpleasant

I would like to share with you some aspects of a mirror-like mind for you to apply to your own experience, your own situation in life. A mirror reflects what is considered beautiful just as something that is beautiful. For example, a flower comes before a mirror and the mirror would reflect the flower just as it is. Now think of something that we consider as not so beautiful, not so pleasant, such as a spider—is it a good example? Perhaps it's not good. So a spider would be reflected just as a spider. No discrimination between the flower and the spider.

A Mind like a Mirror

You see how we are trying to apply this in our meditation. We have a pleasant experience: we are aware of the pleasant experience just as it is. We have an unpleasant experience, what we consider as an unpleasant experience, and we reflect it as it is. That is why I have been reminding you many times, if there is a pleasant sensation just know that there is a pleasant sensation. And if there is an unpleasant sensation, can we make friends with it? And can we relate to that without resisting it? Can we be really open to what we consider unpleasant sensations?

And that is why I was also suggesting that when the monsters are there, be open to them, make friends with them. And when they are not there just know that they are not there. This is one aspect of the mirror-like mind and this can be applied to all our life, to all our experience.

So the real challenge you have is that while you are here maybe you are having very pleasant experiences but then, when you go back to your computers in everyday life, when you are having what can be considered as unpleasant experiences, how far can you be open to them? This is the challenge we have. How far can we learn from such experiences? Like learning from the German weather!

I will be speaking more about this as we go along, because many meditators have been telling me that here it is very nice, it is wonderful, it is spacious. But going back is the problem. Monsters are more or less sleeping here, but when we are back in our daily lives, they wake up with a lot of power, a lot of energy. What to do when that happens? I really wish I could create more monsters here for them to practice with! And then I could tell them: Now here are the monsters, see. Can you make friends with them? Can you learn from them? Anyway, this is the first point about what we can describe as the mirror-like mind.

Letting Go of Experiences

Another important aspect of a mirror-like mind is that nothing is retained. Things are reflected just as they are. Nothing is taken in. Now this touches on the greatest problem we have in everyday life. Especially when we have unpleasant experiences, we give them minuses and then we take them in. And we are very good at accumulating things, collecting things, and we are excellent in collecting and accumulating these unpleasant experiences. I meet very spiritual people, I meet very good people, but when I talk to them they are very unhappy because they do not see the positive side, but what they are seeing more and more is the minuses, the unpleasant experiences. So this is why I have been emphasising that it is alright that we are carrying these wounds, but let us try to heal them. Let us learn to let go of them. Otherwise we are just holding onto whatever experiences we have been having. And it is interesting to reflect why we are holding on to them, why we carrying the past as a burden in this way, and why we are using this to inflict suffering on ourselves and of course thereby inflicting suffering on others.

This matter of carrying things as a burden is shown in a very well known Zen story: There were two monks who were walking together and they met a beautiful girl standing beside a river. One of the monks realised that the girl was finding it difficult to get across the river, so he carried her across and left her on the other side. Then the following day the other monk said: You know, you did something very wrong, you should be given a big minus because you carried that beautiful girl across the water—do you not know that monks cannot touch women? And the other monk said: I have left her behind on the other shore—but you are still carrying her!

So that is what we are doing. We cannot just put our experiences down. We are really still carrying them. And I think as we are still human, it is natural that we carry them, it is natural that we hold on to them. But we should learn to look at them, maybe to learn from them. They can be extremely valuable experiences and we should see what we can learn from them. And then can we put them down? Can we heal the wounds that we are carrying? Otherwise, as I said, with these wounds you inflict suffering on yourself, and perhaps you might also be inflicting suffering on others. So you have to make a choice, you have to be clear. Do I work with this? Do I learn not to inflict suffering on myself and not to inflict suffering on others by healing these wounds? This is the second aspect of the mirror-like mind.

Neither Accepting nor Rejecting

A third aspect which we can relate to in our everyday life—seeing how the mirror-like mind functions—is that the mirror-like mind does not accept things nor does it reject things. Without accepting, without rejecting, it is just allowing, just being, with whatever is happening. This is why I gave you an exercise to work with the reacting mind and the non-reacting mind. Again, as we are still human we have this tendency to accept, to reject, to like, to dislike, plus, minus—we are still human so it is not surprising that we do this. It is natural that we like the Sri Lankan weather and that we do not like the German weather. But then you realise that we have no control over the Sri Lankan weather and over the German weather. I cannot demand: I would like to have only Sri Lankan weather, I do not want German weather anymore!

You are amused, but this is exactly what we do in life. Wanting things in another way. My business should be working in this way. My girl-friend should be behaving this way. I should be behaving this way. Demanding things from ourselves, demanding things from others, demanding things from life, like demanding Sri Lankan weather. Demanding is one thing, what is happening is another thing. And after demanding Sri Lankan weather in the morning, I have to work with the German weather in the afternoon!

Supposing I was identifying with the Sri Lankan weather, I would be depressed by now. Oh, the Sri Lankan weather is gone! When will it come again? Waiting in hope for the Sri Lankan weather to come. Can we not apply this to what happens in everyday life? Again, as I am human, it is natural that I am longing for Sri Lankan weather all the time so that I can throw this coat away. This shows the importance of reflection. I have to stop and reflect: Now, is my demand reasonable? When I make this demand, am I being realistic? Is it possible? Are we always getting what we are demanding?

And with this kind of reflection we realise the nature of our actions, the nature of our demands. We need only to see this, to understand this, and from that seeing, from that understanding, realisation can come. So I have to realise I cannot make demands. I have to see how far I can make friends with the German weather. How far can I see the beauty in the German weather? How far can I learn from the German weather? How far can I make discoveries about the German weather? Then you realise that you can see certain things which you had not seen before because your depression has gone.

Do you realise that what we are doing with more and more meditation is creating more and more space in our mind, creating more and more clarity in our mind, having more and more awareness, so that we can see what we are doing? Then we come to a state where when the German weather is there it is nice, it is interesting. This is difficult, it is a challenge. If the Sri Lankan weather comes, that is fine. But if it does not come, the German weather is also fine. Need we go further? Is the message not clear? I can speak more about the mirror-like mind, but is this necessary? Isn't this clear enough to see where you are, at least to realise what you have to do? So while you are here you are having Sri Lankan weather, when you go back you will have German weather. And when you are there please do not demand Sri Lankan weather! That's it!

* * *

Guided Meditation : Choiceless Awareness

Now please allow the mind to do what it likes. Let any thoughts arise, thoughts about the past, thoughts about the future. And let us learn to observe the thoughts without judging them, no plus, no minus, just thoughts arising and thoughts passing away; but please be alert, awake from moment-to-moment. Learning to make friends with our thoughts, learning to create space for our thoughts.

For those who have problems with thoughts, please learn that there is nothing wrong with thoughts if you can be aware, if you can know what thoughts are arising and passing away.

In this meditation you don't try to stop thoughts, you don't try to control thoughts, you create space for any thought to arise. What you are learning now is to develop a non-reactive mind in relation to thoughts.

Now let us learn to make friends with the emotions that we don't like. So please allow those emotions that you don't like to arise and see, as with the thoughts, whether you can make friends with them, create space around them, just allow them to be there.

If anyone is feeling sleepy or drowsy, please open your eyes because it is very important to be alert, to be awake. It is very important for us to learn not to push away, not to control unpleasant emotions, but to allow them to arise and to make friends with them and to create space for them. Let us learn this very important aspect.

Let us now learn to do the same in relation to unpleasant sensation. Allow the unpleasant sensations in the body to arise. What you consider as strange feelings, unusual feelings, what you consider as abnormal sensations, let them arise. It can be in any part of the body. Can we learn to relate to these sensations without giving a minus, to relate to them as just sensations?

Thoughts, emotions, sensations, learning to see them just as they are, learning to relate to them without a plus, without a minus. This is learning to have loving-kindness to our thoughts, to our emotions, to our sensations. Then they don't become problems for us. Then they become our friends. This is what we are trying to do with this meditation.

Part Two

PRACTICE IN DAILY LIFE

9
WORKING WITH EMOTIONS

Today I would like to discuss how to work with emotions in the context of meditation, especially the emotions that can create suffering for us. Maybe it would be interesting to list the emotions we do not like—for example, aggression. Anything else? A bad mood, feeling lazy, being indifferent, giving up, anxiety, insecurity, doubts, mental pain, sadness, panic, antipathy, pressure, confusion, not being awake, feeling guilty. We are all familiar with these, we all have experience of these. Is there anyone who likes them?

Retreatant: Sometimes.

Godwin: But not most of the time, I think this is the issue. Because I think even as children we have been taught or influenced, in a way, to see these emotions as bad, that we should not be having them, we should not be experiencing them. In this connection there is a very interesting book that came out recently called 'Emotional Intelligence'. Has anyone heard of it? It has been written by Daniel Goleman, an American Buddhist. And it has become a best-seller within a very short time—that shows that emotions are a big issue! He makes some very interesting points. One is that having a high IQ is considered something very important. Goleman says this is nonsense, even if you have a low IQ, if you show some intelligence towards the emotions, that is more important than having a high IQ.

Another important point that he makes is why he thought of writing this book. He found that in America young children are becoming more and more violent and aggressive, and have some of the negative emotions that we have mentioned. But they are not taught how to work with these emotions. So perhaps, as a result of that book, some schools, some education authorities are thinking of ways and means of educating children so they know how to work with emotions intelligently.

This is related to the point I was making before that, as children, we have been conditioned to hate our emotions, to repress them, to deny them and so on, and then we grow up with this idea that they are bad, that they are wrong, that we should not experience them. This is a strong conditioning that we have and then, in addition to that, when we take to meditation and the spiritual life, we are also told that anger is bad. Then all these positions about emotions create a kind of split between what you should be and what you are. So then the spiritual life also becomes a battle—a battle of emotions, and meditators find they really hate themselves.

This is the first point I want to make, which is not easy: to learn to be open to these emotions. What I am going to share with you is based on my own experiences and understanding of the Dhamma, after working with meditators for many years. What I have discovered over the years I call *tools*: tools to work with these emotions. I have already mentioned the first tool, which is learning to be open to them—learning to say OK to them, learning not to give very strong minuses to them. I must say this is not easy, but this is very important. And this is the first tool.

INVESTIGATING EMOTIONS

The second tool is related to that, and it is to learn about them, to discover about them—as it is said in the Dhamma, to investigate them. To really investigate them, to work with them, in the first place we have to really experience them. How can you work with them if you do not realise that you are experiencing them? If you can fully experience them, then once you know that they are there, finding out, learning, discovering, exploring is very interesting. And there are very different emotions, as we mentioned, each emotion is something special, so that we can learn something different from each of them.

Yesterday anger was mentioned. Let us take this emotion as an example, because I think we all can relate to it very easily. When anger comes, you must say: Wonderful! I am going to learn from this anger. And then you try to find out: "Now what causes the anger? What is the reason for this anger?" When you explore in this way, what might you learn?

Retreatant: Bad thoughts cause the anger.

Godwin: I think we can all relate to that experience. You have an expectation of how the other person should behave—this is very important. It is natural that we expect people to behave in the way we think that he or she should behave, and we should see this as very interesting. To discover: "Ah, I get angry because I have this idea how others should behave." So when you get angry, if you can learn to see that, realise that, then you can be with the *anger* rather than with the *person* who is creating the anger; watching what exactly is happening inside your mind. If you can do that, actually the anger can become an object of meditation.

Perhaps another tool related to that is not to repress it, not to push it away, and not to indulge it, but just *to be with* the anger, with that awareness. And what is more fascinating and more interesting is to find out what is happening in our body when there is anger. Here again you can see the importance of awareness. If you can learn to be aware of these sensations, these experiences, whatever you experience in the body with the anger, what is interesting is that there is no more build up. This is because I think what happens with most of these emotions is that there is a build up with thoughts, and then more emotions arise. But here, just being with the sensations prevents this huge build up.

You can do this exploration, this investigation, this discovery, in relation to any emotion and you will learn how each single emotion is different from the other, but at the same time there is also an interesting pattern to all of them; and to discover the pattern is fascinating.

Now an interesting practical question arises in everyday life. Does this mean that you allow everyone to behave in his own way, and then you look at your own anger and you do nothing else about it? Is that a solution? What do you think of that solution?

☙ **Retreatant:** It can be dangerous.

❀ **Godwin:** The point I am making is that if you are always passive and just watching, this can be easily exploited by others. They say: "He is a meditator, you can do anything with him. He will only look at his breath. He will just investigate it. So you can do anything to him." This is the challenge we have in everyday life. There are times when you have to assert yourself, when you have to be honest and communicate this to other people. This is an aspect of the second tool. The first tool is being open to it, braving the conditioning we have; and the second tool is exploring, investigating, learning and so on.

Experiencing Emotions as They Are

The third tool, which I consider extremely important, is that when these emotions are not there, to know that they are not there. We have given them such power, such energy that when they are not there we are hardly aware that they are not there. I would consider this as a real tragedy in the human condition. There are moments when we are free, but it is too good to believe that we can be free. Some people come to me and say: Maybe I am repressing them! It is really funny that we have this reaction, this position in relation to these emotions.

In this connection Thich Nhat Hanh says something very beautiful, which I like very much. He says: "When you have a toothache you suffer from it, so when you do not have one why can't you say: 'Wow! I have no toothache!' and enjoy that?" That is a very simple, practical, direct teaching which comes from the Dhamma itself. This is very much emphasised in the Dhamma: to know when the emotions are there and to know when they are not there. When they are there to use the tools, and when they are not there, just being with their absence.

Another very strong conditioning we have is that when they are not there we give it a big plus, and when the emotions are there we give it a big minus. So we have to slowly, slowly learn not to give a minus, not to give a plus. As I said this morning: just being, just learning to reflect things just as they are.

Making Friends with Emotions

Another tool which I have mentioned very often is making friends with these emotions. Because as I said earlier, due to our conditioning we hate them, we really dislike them. And it would be a very good experience if you can see for yourself that by hating them, by disliking them, not wanting them to be there, you give them more power and more energy.

There is a very interesting story in Buddhism, which presents this important aspect in the form of an allegory. It seems there was a demon and this demon would live on other peoples' anger. So you can just imagine that he had enough food! And he had food wherever he went: Sri Lankan food, German food ... The demon eventually got tired with the same food he was always getting, and he wanted to taste something new. So he thought of visiting the gods to find out whether he would starve or whether he would get divine food.

Then, as the story goes, he went to the world of the gods, and as he entered there was a security officer of the gods. And the security officer got angry, so the demon got the first taste of divine food and he liked it very much! Then he went inside to find out more about that place. There he found the throne of the chief god empty and he went and sat on the throne. Then some gods saw this and said "There's a demon sitting on the boss's seat;" and the gods also got angry. But something very interesting happened because when the demon first sat on the throne he was very small, but the more the gods got angry the bigger the demon became!

By then the chief of the gods knew that something was happening, so he came and he saw this demon on the throne. He spoke to the demon in a very friendly way, welcoming him and showing him every kindness, and, of course, the demon started to shrink as there was no food for him to feed on! So when working with a person having strong emotions, I would say: Just invite the emotions and see what happens, and then I would urge the person to do that from time to time so as to get used to it.

Then another tool would be that sometimes I would get people to sketch their monsters, and even just by sketching these things they would become nervous, they would become insecure. So the principle is that by making friends with them, saying OK to them, when they come unexpectedly the power and the energy that we have given them is less.

Dealing with Fear and Phobias

This brings up a very interesting point, that in relation to working with fear, phobias and similar emotions the practice is not to move away from them. When you move away from them you give them more power and energy; but instead you should slowly, slowly experiment with them, explore them. This is a very important practice in the Dhamma. One way you could use it is that when you have fear, you deliberately and consciously expose yourself to fearful situations and watch these fears. I know young monks in Thailand and in Tibet, who would go and spend a night with their teacher in the cemetery. So it becomes a learning experience, to see what happens in that situation. It is related to this principle of inviting the monsters, bringing them up.

Another tool is when you are having an emotion, see if you can take away the word and then just be with what you are really experiencing without the word—please try this. Sometimes we have become victims of words, of concepts. The other day someone was telling me that he was feeling depressed. When I questioned that person, asking what exactly his experience was when he was depressed, he said: I am having negative thoughts about myself, and am giving minuses to the thoughts. Now just this process of giving minuses to the thoughts he was calling depression. Take away the word 'depression' and just watch this process of giving minuses.

There is one last tool which comes from a meditation technique which is called *noting*. You can try this. It is very interesting. Just use a word, just label whatever it is that you are experiencing. You do not control it. You do not try to push it away. You have knowledge very honestly of what is happening, and you just say: Sadness, sadness; fear, fear; thoughts, thoughts; or sensations, sensations.

I think there are about 7 or 8 tools I have given you now. So I would like to pause here, and if you have any questions, any difficulties, please ask them, because this is a very important theme, especially in everyday life. Because on retreat, generally speaking, the monsters are sleeping. Everyone is practising loving-kindness. Everyone is smiling. The bell goes and you get good meals. There is beautiful nature all around. It is easy to put the monsters to sleep, but when you go back home, they really wake up. This is why before they wake up I am giving you the tools.

*   *   *

Discussion

Retreatant: What to do if many different monsters are coming up at the same time?

Godwin: Some people might say, I cannot handle even two or three! This brings up a very important point of how these monsters are related. They are all one family. Let us take one emotion as an example: anger. When there is anger you can also have guilt. When you have guilt there is another emotion that arises, and so on—they are all related, they come as a team and they work very well as a team, they are very powerful.

Retreatant: Perhaps you can give them a ball to play with.

Godwin: That is one of the solutions. I am happy you mentioned this idea of playing. And when you play you learn you can't always win: sometimes they win, sometimes you win. When they win, do not give a minus, when you win, do not give a plus—just see it as a fact. Here again, what is important is just to have friendliness. The phrase that you can use is: I do not feel OK with all these monsters, but it is OK not to feel OK.

And when there are so many and you are overwhelmed by them it is not possible to have even a little space. But there will be a time when you recover from them. Maybe after one day, maybe after two days, maybe after three weeks. Then you can take your mind back and reflect: now what really happened to me? What is the mechanism by which this family of monsters come together? I must understand their secret. So this becomes an exploration, an investigation—but again, in a very friendly way, to just understand them. You honestly say: "Now last time they won. Let me wait for the next time when they come." Then you are really waiting with friendliness, with an open mind: when are they coming, how are they coming?

This is a paradox: when you are open to them, waiting for them, they do not come. This principle is again presented in the Dhamma in a beautiful way. According to the Dhamma, the biggest monster is Mara. It is Mara, according to Buddhist terms, who is bringing up these different monsters in different ways. And it is said that Mara really likes people to fight with him, because when you fight with Mara he becomes very powerful. So again you should just say: "There you are, Mara. It is okay that you are there, Mara." Then he becomes very insecure.

Using Different Techniques

Retreatant: There is one technique where we are not using words, and another technique where we are labelling—isn't this a little contradictory?

Godwin: So they seem contradictory. This is why I offer many tools—for some, the noting technique helps; and for others, they need to drop the words. For some, when they use the word they get some distance. But for another, when they drop the words they get the same distance. This is why I give you different techniques, because for different people, depending where they are at, you have to use different techniques, and find out which one is the most effective for you. That raises a very important point: the principle is that you do not give anything special importance. You just see it as another thing that is happening—that is a very interesting principle.

Retreatant: Should I also use the labelling technique for positive emotions?

Godwin: This is why I said when these unpleasant emotions are not there just to know that they are not there. And then eventually you will see no difference whether they are there or whether they are not there.

Retreatant: Are there positive aspects of so-called negative emotions?

Godwin: In other words, can so-called negative emotions have a positive aspect? A very important point to reflect upon. There are stories in the Buddhist text where people have had these negative emotions and they made them the object of meditation and that has helped them to become enlightened. So no plus, no minus. States of mind arise, states of mind pass away. Just seeing them as they are.

Retreatant: You said earlier that we should not give labels to emotions. So how do we observe the emotions?

Godwin: Very good, practical question. I like such questions. Suppose you are experiencing boredom, then you take away the word boredom and find out what you are actually experiencing. Is it a sensation that you are calling boredom? Is it a particular thought that you are considering as boredom? Is it a particular feeling which you have categorised as boredom? So when we can explore like this, boredom can become very interesting.

Retreatant: Your advice is that we should not label emotions with words, and you have already told us that if there is no anger, just to know there is no anger. But when we say there is no anger we are putting words to describe a certain experience, so isn't that contradictory?

❁ **Godwin:** Very good question. I like that question. If you consider the tools, you'll see that sometimes we need to use words, sometimes we don't have to use words. This is why there are a variety of tools, so if one doesn't work you can experiment with the others. What is important is that you have to find out which tools are really helping you. Once you discover the tools that are helping you, you have to use them.

It's interesting that these tools are related to each person individually. We human beings have different conditionings, different personalities. This is why I have been trying to present tools which can cover all types of human beings. So the last point I want to make is that it is very important in the spiritual path, in meditation, for you to experiment, for you to find out for yourself. The Buddha emphasised this very much, to be self-reliant, to be your own teacher, to be a light to yourself.

Dealing with Powerful Emotions

☙ **Retreatant:** How can I handle very powerful emotions?

❁ **Godwin:** The unfortunate thing is that if you fear something, if you do not want something, that can be a way to invite it to come. Here again the solution may be not to give these particular emotions a lot of power, a lot of energy, but to see no difference between these particular emotions and other emotions, and to be sure of the tools that you are using in working with these emotions. This is one point.

The second point is, it is very interesting that from the Buddhist point of view depression has a strong element of self-hatred. So you see with more and more meditation of loving-kindness—this is why I have been emphasising this meditation technique so often—that with more and more practice of this meditation you can be almost certain that such states of mind will not arise, and even if they do arise, if you can really have loving-kindness towards them, again their power and energy become less.

And the third point is that by using these tools more and more you develop self-confidence. And this self-confidence is extremely important because it helps you come to a position where any state of mind may arise, but, as you know the tools, there is no problem. And if that can really happen then you come to a state of mind where whether these emotions are there or whether they are not there makes no difference. That I would consider as a breakthrough. So this is how we should practice meditation, in this practical way.

Retreatant: We shouldn't put labels to our emotions, but if I have anger and I put it down, how am I supposed to observe it? If I do not have the emotion how can I observe it?

Godwin: Supposing we are working with anger. I think anger is a common emotion that we can all relate to. Then, when we don't have anger, just to know: Ah, I don't have anger now. You can take your mind backwards and see that the whole of this morning you did not get angry. At the end of the day you might say: Oh, today, the whole day I was free of anger. You'll be surprised what a good person you have been and then you'll feel more and more positive about this.

Retreatant: With such emotions it's never too late to want revenge. Sometimes you can put it down and forgive but it arises again, so what can you do about it?

Godwin: Good question, because again we can relate to such an experience. I would like to offer some suggestions how to work with such situations. The first suggestion is: don't be surprised. This is the way with emotions, sometimes they don't come, and then sometimes they come. So when they come, please don't be surprised. When emotions go we come to the conclusion: "Now it is all over." But the problem is with our conclusion that they should not come again.

The second suggestion is when they arise to be aware of them and to use the different tools but without giving yourself a minus. This is what is important. But arising from that question I would like to emphasise something very important, which is that you should not, as I said, come to the conclusion that you will not be having these emotions again, but rather, when they come, see if you can feel grateful for them, see if you can see them as an opportunity, if you can learn from them. Then, as I said earlier, you come to a state where whether they come or whether they don't come makes no difference. So that is what we should try to aim at rather than reach the conclusion that now they are over.

According to the Buddhist teachings, these things completely stop only when we have become enlightened. But as I said yesterday, we are trying to be enlightened people even before we are enlightened! This brings up a point that I have been emphasising very much in my talks: learning to accept our humanness, learning to accept our imperfections. It is very important in our practice.

Retreatant: I want to know how to deal with sadness. Sometimes one just can't let it go because you can even feel it in dreams, particularly when relatives pass away.

Godwin: I don't want to go over the tools again. I would like to repeat that whether it is sadness, whether it is fear, whether it is anxiety, whether it is guilt, it is the same medicine. But this shows that the sadness has become fairly deep and that it even comes up in a dream. But please remember, please be open to the days when you don't dream about sadness. When the sadness is not there, just to be aware that the sadness is not there.

There might be two types of sadness. One type of sadness is in relation to a particular incident. There may be another type of sadness which is not related to an incident, but you just generally feel sadness. If it is related to a particular incident, that incident should become an object of meditation. To see clearly that that experience of sadness has been created by your expectations of how things should have been.

And if it is just sadness that comes without a reason, what you might try to do is to feel the sensations in the body while you are experiencing the sadness, because with sadness sometimes our thoughts can make it worse. So if you can be with the sensations, this may be helpful.

Another tool, as I have been mentioning a few times, is to come back to your breath because it is happening now. It is interesting that all sadness is in relation to the past. Sadness is in relation to the past and anxiety is in relation to the future. So making a connection with your breath and learning to be in the present helps us to handle the past and the future. By doing that we learn to handle these emotions which are always related to the past and the future. And in conclusion I would like to again mention one of the tools that I referred to earlier: when sadness is not there try to invite sadness and you might find that it will not come.

Retreatant: Can mind-power be as strong and firm as a stone?

Godwin: I wouldn't want to liken it to a stone. I would say that rather than seeing it as a stone it should be seen as something warm, it should be seen as something gentle, soft, tender. These are the spiritual qualities that come with the practice. This is completely different from a stone which is something with no feelings. Something beautiful about human beings is that we have this ability to feel, and we should allow this feeling to arise, but then this feeling should be worked with, it has to be understood.

Now let us take a short break and during the break I would like to suggest that you reflect on some of the tools that I have mentioned and then discover for yourself what emotions are bothering you. It is very important to learn to reflect on such themes. Reflection is thinking about a particular theme, and when you think about it, if other thoughts come you should learn to let go of them and come back to the theme that you are really reflecting on. So I would like you to do this. It doesn't matter whether you are walking or sitting or whatever you are doing, just to learn to develop this important meditation of reflecting.

* * *

GUIDED MEDITATION ON EMOTIONS

Now let us do a meditation relating to what we have been discussing. Those who have problems with unpleasant emotions, please allow them to arise now.

If these emotions that we don't like arise, let us see how far we can make friends with them. Let us see how far we can just allow them, just let them be. Just to relate to them as a visitor who has come.

And if you don't have any unpleasant emotions, just to know that you don't have any unpleasant emotions.

Can we learn to relate to them without giving them a minus?

Can you really say to yourself, it is okay not to feel okay?

Can you feel grateful that this emotion is there so that you can learn to work with it?

Can you now have the self-confidence that if these emotions come again you know how to work with them, you know how to handle them?

Now please open your eyes.

[End of meditation]

We can do some nice chanting now. Actually chanting is also a very powerful tool to work with emotions, especially if you can be completely in the present while you are chanting. Please see for yourself how chanting will help you. It will help you to create space in your mind.

10
HOW WE CREATE SUFFERING: GIVING PLUSSES AND MINUSES

We can ask ourselves: About whom am I thinking? Most of the time we are thinking about ourselves, everything is related to us. Isn't this very fascinating? Even when we are thinking about others, it is always related to ourselves. And then we do something more interesting. What do we do when we are thinking of ourselves and others?

- **Retreatant:** We think how we would like others to be.
- **Godwin:** Very good. Right, what else do we do?
- **Retreatant:** We compare.
- **Godwin:** We compare.
- **Retreatant:** We have doubts about ourselves.
- **Retreatant:** We think how things can be useful to ourselves.
- **Godwin:** Yes, right.
- **Retreatant:** We emotionally make judgements about others.
- **Godwin:** Wonderful, excellent. You put it so clearly. And the phrase that I use is: we give plusses, we give minuses. Please see it for yourself. Good things that you remember about yourself—plus. Good things you think of another person—plus for him. Bad things, wrong things you have done—minus. Wrong things, bad things others have done—minus. The people I meet who suffer the most are most of the time giving themselves minuses. Such a person can create a hell for themselves, and in that hell only minuses exist. Minuses about ourselves, minuses about others, minuses about the world. When that happens we use a very common word, we say: I suffer from depression.

So you see the connection between plusses, minuses and emotions? Isn't this interesting? Isn't this fascinating? Shouldn't we find it curious? Isn't meditation something very worthwhile? Isn't there an element of lightness in it? Isn't this an adventure? Isn't this the most beautiful adventure we can have, understanding, exploring, investigating, as I said this morning, the inner world?

DIFFICULTIES IN RELATIONSHIPS

It was a learning experience for me listening to your problems regarding emotions. It is clear to me that emotions arise in connection with the way you relate to yourself, the way you relate to others, and the way you relate to your surroundings. This shows that relationships are a real challenge we have in life. Many persons presented problems relating to other people. So their problem was that they were concerned about what others were thinking of them—especially fearing minuses. Then the question arises: Why have we given such power to other people that our happiness and unhappiness is dependent on them? I would like to raise this as a question: Why have we given so much power to other people?

Retreatant: If one has no self-confidence, one does not know how to get hold of one's destiny.

Godwin: I think this seems to be an important reason. Because we lack self-confidence, because we don't practise what is necessary for this, we depend on other people for it. Another point that arose in my mind today was—at least among the people I have been speaking with in this regard—only women have been telling me that how they relate to other people creates this sense of lack of self-confidence, fearing the judgement of others, fearing to make mistakes where others will blame them. Now a question that arose in my mind is that here in this country, is this most commonly experienced by women, or do men also have this problem but are they too shy to speak about it?

How We Create Suffering: Giving Plusses and Minuses

ೞ Retreatant: Men have more of this kind of problem. Men know how to find ways to let out their emotions: for example, they will go out to drink with friends and when they get a bit drunk, they will just say anything, then they just let out the emotions in this way or some other.

❀ Godwin: I think everywhere in this world this is a real problem human beings have to face. I didn't know that with men one of the solutions they have found is drinking, but then it becomes a vicious circle: because of their drinking they are also given minuses and because of the minuses they drink, so one thing leads to the other.

Let us see how meditation helps us to work with these problems. Whether it is in men or women, it doesn't matter. I feel this is why meditation of loving-kindness is so important, in the sense that you learn to be your own best friend. And if you can really make that connection with yourself, actually feel it, then I think your dependency on what others think of you becomes less, because whatever you need from others you get it from yourself. You will become self-contained within yourself.

Another way meditation helps us to work with this situation is through understanding the nature of plusses and minuses. It is very interesting that human beings have this very strong conditioning to give plusses or to give minuses in any situation, but we never pause to question whether these plusses or minuses are valid, or ask on what basis are we doing this.

It is funny, we really become victims of this mechanism but we never inquire into the way these plusses and minuses operate, under what condition they arise, what is really creating them, what is contributing to them. So when we explore this question we realise that these are really related to thoughts, concepts, which have come, due to various reasons, from the society that we have been brought up in. Then you see them as part of your conditioning, you see them as a strong habit that we have got used to.

It is funny that this is how we use thoughts. Now, as we all know, from the time that we wake up in the morning up to the time that we go to sleep there are continuous thoughts going through our mind which never stop. If you become aware, if you become mindful of the thoughts that go through your mind, then you'll realise that most of the time the way we use thoughts is in this habit of giving plusses and minuses. So when you see this clearly, then the power that we have given to them may become less.

Then you realise that sometimes it is just an innocent thought that comes: maybe the other person doesn't like me; maybe the other person is giving me minuses; maybe the other person thinks that I'm silly or ridiculous, and so on. But if you are mindful you'll realise it is just a thought that you're having. Who knows whether that thought corresponds to any reality? There is a strong imaginary aspect in our thoughts. This imaginary aspect and the reality are two different things. So with awareness, with mindfulness, by exploring and investigating, this may become clear to us and this will help us to work with and handle such thoughts, and their power will become less.

Another very interesting aspect related to this is: with our thoughts, with our identifications, we all have images of who we are, the type of persons we are. Each person has a model, has an image of himself or herself. I think what we are doing is that when other people accept our image then we feel comfortable with them, we feel at ease with them. And then we make it a point to always, or most of the time, impose this particular image on other people. Then we also have images of other people. A Western psychologist has said that when two people meet, there are six people. Can you work out how two people become six people?

Retreatant: There are two real people, and four imaginary people: who you think you are, and who you think the other person is; who the other person thinks he is, and who he thinks you are!

Godwin: Yes, exactly. It is a very interesting point for us to reflect on. Sometimes when there are conflicts actually it is the images that are in conflict, but what the people really are is

How We Create Suffering: Giving Plusses and Minuses

another question. So with meditation, with awareness, you understand this process, that whenever there is a conflict, the conflict is the result of the image you have of the other person.

Take the case of anger. In relation to the behaviour of another person how do we get angry? Why do we get angry? We have an idea of how the other person should behave and when the other person's behaviour does not conform to the image we have, we get angry. Then we have an image of our usual behaviour, and when our behaviour does not correspond to that image then we feel guilty, we get angry, we get disappointed, we get hurt because our behaviour does not correspond to the image we have formed of ourselves.

A very interesting practice in everyday life is, whenever you suffer, whenever you are disappointed, whenever you are frustrated, at that moment can you see for yourself that the image which you have is now clashing with what is actually happening? This is why the Buddha emphasised learning to see things as they are. But what we are doing is, we want to see things the way they should be, as they must be according to our way, my way.

What we are doing is making demands about how we should behave, we are making demands about how others should behave, and we are making demands about how life should be. If these demands are met, life is okay, life is wonderful, it is beautiful. If these demands are not met, there is suffering, frustration, disappointment, hurt; and most of these emotions can arise as a result of that. So I would suggest that an enlightened human being goes through life without any images, and because of that he or she can never suffer.

Another aspect related to this is, if you can really understand the nature of life, then you realise it is not possible to form any conclusion about how life should be. In the Dhamma there is something very deep, which is to be open to the uncertainty of life. But we hold onto this idea of certainty because we assume things can be controlled. But when we think deeply we realise that in actual fact we have no control.

In cultures and in countries where things work perfectly, without any problems, this gives a kind of sense of security because everything is happening perfectly, no problems, everything is under control. Living in countries like India or Sri Lanka, you have to be open to uncertainties. I will give a practical example which I experienced myself. When I was in Europe I was on a train and they made an announcement in the language of that country and people were very anxious, looking at their leaflets and there was lots of talk about it, lots of disappointment, so I asked them what the announcement was about. They said the train was going to be seven minutes late. In Sri Lanka, if there is a train at all you'll be very fortunate!

So this is a very good training. Most of the time unexpected things happen. You go to the bus stand and then they say: "No bus today." You want to go by train, they say: "Now there is no train, it is one hour late." I get the impression that these things don't happen here. Am I right? Everything is under control, and it gives a sense of security; then when something unexpected happens there is disappointment, suffering.

Living in cultures like this naturally you tend to be conditioned to do things perfectly. You fear to make mistakes because no mistakes should happen! With this idea of perfection, this is why you like other people to accept that you are perfect, this is why you fear maybe they are giving you minuses, because your model of perfection is affected by that. This is why I often emphasise this being open to our humanness, open to our imperfections, so that when we become more and more open to our humanness, our imperfections, then if you are getting minuses from other people then you are not surprised. You realise, well, that's part of our conditioning: I'm still human, so it's okay.

* * *

How We Create Suffering: Giving Plusses and Minuses

Discussion

I would like to pause now and I'm sure you might have some questions, or need some clarifications about this, so I think we will try to have a useful discussion about our emotions and how to really work with our emotions in the context of the practice. It is interesting that when it comes to asking questions, you are afraid: "Could this be a good question? Will people laugh at my question? Will they think I'm stupid?" But here we are in a group of spiritual friends so we should try be open to anything, allow ourselves to make mistakes and learn from these mistakes: this is the beauty of a retreat like this. So I would like to hear some silly questions, and I will be happy to give some silly answers!

Retreatant: In Hong Kong we have a certain set of images to live by and we always do things in conformity with these images. For example, if we go to a cafe and order a certain type of Chinese tea but the waiter gives us another type, if we accept the wrong tea the important thing is whether we accept it with or without a grudge.

Godwin: That is certainly true. We can accept it because we want to conform to others, so we pretend it is OK and we accept it. But I think the real acceptance is: Can we really say OK to it, or perhaps not even saying OK, but just seeing it as it is?

Retreatant: My statement is: If I really accept it, the acceptance must either be with a grudge or with understanding, not simply out of conformity.

Retreatant: Master, if we practise giving ourselves all the plusses, seeing the good side in ourselves all the time, where is the line to be drawn?

Godwin: When we have got used to giving minuses, when we have got used to seeing the unpleasant elements in us, when we are relating to ourselves as an enemy, how do we work with this situation? This is the important issue. So in such a situation just to realise: "I'm only giving minuses to myself; aren't there good things that I've done?" Then we are learning to see the good things, factually, objectively, without, of course, being conceited about it, but simply as a fact.

Then we learn to see the goodness, we learn to see the positive side, we learn to see things as they are, as the Buddha said. This is the important thing. Then, as I said, we learn to see the goodness in others which helps us to appreciate them. Also when you see goodness in others, learning to rejoice in it. So in this way you learn very important spiritual qualities which are helping your practice.

Dealing with Pressure from Others

What are the emotions that come up in everyday life? Let us discuss the ways and means in which meditation can help us to cope with emotions in such daily situations.

Retreatant: I would like to give one example: in my office I always try to work to conform to what my clients expect me to do. It's not because I care how they judge me. Actually I don't care as long as I've done my job right, then I'm happy. But the reality is that if I don't do things in conformity with their expectations they will complain to me which results in spending a lot of time explaining the situation. So that gives me a lot of pressure. I know that it is all created by my mind and I can handle the situation if there should be any unjustified complaints, but the fact is that I try to avoid these troubles, so I try to do everything perfectly.

Godwin: Good point, a big plus to you. What I would suggest is that what I'm saying doesn't mean that you should not act with responsibility. One thing we have to learn is how to act with responsibility but without the pressure. You are doing your best but doing your best is done in a relaxed way, not with tension, not with stress. This is one thing we need to learn. And then when you do your best and still you have made a mistake, then you can be very clear and honest in your own mind: I did my best, but my best was not good enough for the other person, so what can I do? At least it makes your mind very clear, it makes your conscience very clear, so that it will not give rise to any inner conflicts.

This is all we can try to do; and when we have tried, if it succeeds, it is good. If it fails, it is also good. And then in such a situation, if you have made a mistake and then some problem arises, what is also important for us to learn is that when a wound has been created, to heal that wound as quickly as possible rather than just hold onto the wound and suffer for your whole life because you have made some mistakes. Anything else?

Retreatant: But in Hong Kong you may be fired by the boss. That is the source of the pressure.

Godwin: If you have done your best and if you're fired, still in your own mind you can be very clear about what has happened. I feel it is very important in life to understand our limitations. This doesn't mean that we justify our limitations, but that it is a fact: I'm doing my very best but my very best does not correspond to what others think of as best, so what can I do? Actually, these are the real challenges we have in life: how to face them?

NOT HAVING EXPECTATIONS

Another aspect of such situations—I don't know if what I'm going to say makes sense to you—some of these setbacks, some of these difficulties, some of these problems you have in such situations can later on prove to be a blessing. This is also very interesting. I'm reminded of a Chinese tale that I would like to share with you; perhaps you already know the story. In a particular village there was a very wise old man and he had some beautiful horses. One day one of the beautiful horses was missing, it had run away. So the whole village came to this man and said: "Oh, how unfortunate it is that your best horse has run away. It seems you are very unlucky." Maybe in Buddhist terms we would say it is bad kamma, and so on. He said: "No, it is merely that my horse has run away. What you are saying is an opinion, judgement, about what has happened. My horse has run away, that's all, no need to give a minus about this."

Then after some days this horse came back with another beautiful horse. Then the same villagers came and said: "Oh, you're very lucky, you're very fortunate, you lost one horse, now you have two horses." He said: "Stop all this, I now have two horses, that is all, no need to give a plus." This old man had a son, and the son was trying to train this new horse, and in training the new horse he fell from the horse and broke his leg. So his friends came and said: Bad kamma again.

And then there was a war and soldiers came to the village to take away all the young people in the village to fight in the war, only the old man's son was saved from this because of his broken leg! This is a very good story to learn to see things just as they are, hopefully without plusses and without minuses. I suppose the wise old man did not have any image of what should happen and what shouldn't happen.

So, no images, this is one point. The other point is, when there is a shift that takes place inside us, when there is understanding and realisation inside, anything can happen externally. This is the important thing. We cannot control what is happening externally, but when there is a change inside then you will be able to handle whatever is happening externally. I think this is another aspect of the story.

Dangers of Expecting Perfection

Retreatant: In Hong Kong society even though you can achieve 99% perfection, with the 1% you have committed as a mistake, people will grab hold of that 1% fault and go on and on against you. I fully understand the way you told us how to deal with these situations but I cannot say from the bottom of my heart whether I could do it.

Godwin: I think what you said does not apply only to Hong Kong society. For some reason everywhere in the world there seems to be too much emphasis, too much power, given to the mistakes, to the negative things, and that the good things are taken for granted. This happens very often in relationships. You do good things, and with so many good things you make just one mistake and that one mistake becomes more important than all the good things that you have done. So people will be talking about that one mistake but not at all about the good things that have been done by that person. That brings up the interesting question: Why do human beings give so much power to the mistakes, to the negative things, and the positive things are taken for granted? I would like to hear from you whether you have any thoughts about this.

Retreatant: I think sometimes people only think of the mistake and keep reminding you of it because of jealousy, so they want to magnify the mistake.

Godwin: Anything else? Any other possible explanations?

Retreatant: In my experience it all boils down to greed. It's because, for example, my client expects me to win a legal battle, because if I win the legal battle he will get what he wants. When I do not win the legal battle for him then he has many complaints because his mind is muddled by greed because he does not get what he wants. And the same applies to many other situations that I have seen. When a person has greed in his mind and does not get what he wants, even though I've done my best he won't listen.

Godwin: As we realise that this is something common to ourselves, we should in our own life try to practise in a different way. One suggestion I would like to offer is that whenever we see someone doing something good, I think we should make it a point just to mention it, to appreciate it. For parents who bring up children this is a very common problem, that the parents tell the children only when they make a mistake. When they do something good, that is not mentioned! So a child is brought up with the idea: "I'm always doing wrong."

And this also happens in relationships. Sometimes in Sri Lanka I have to counsel husbands and wives who have problems. It's a big joke amongst my friends. They say this man has no experience in married life and he is counselling married people! One complaint of the wives is that when the cooking is not so good the husband would be critical and make a big fuss about the food, but when the food is good they tell me that the husband practises noble silence!

BEING A SPIRITUAL FRIEND

There is a very interesting discussion in the Buddhist texts about spiritual friends. What a real spiritual friend does is that when someone does something wrong he points it out in a very friendly way that you are doing something wrong; and when they do something good, when they do something right, he points out that you are doing something good, something right.

This is what we need to learn, not only to give power and energy to the minuses but also acknowledge the plusses. So I would suggest that we as meditators should try to cultivate this very important quality. And it is very important to see the good things in ourselves also. This tendency to see only the negative, only the minuses in ourselves is a very strong factor which can create a lot of emotion and suffering for us. But when we learn to see the more and more positive aspects in ourselves, then we will be able to see more and more positive aspects and plusses in others.

There are four qualities mentioned in the Dhamma. They are called Sublime States or Divine Abodes. The first one is loving-kindness, *mettā*. The second one is *karuṇā*, which means compassion, when you see someone suffering you try to help that person. The third quality is very interesting, *muditā*: when other people are happy you rejoice in their happiness, and I would say that you can also rejoice in your own happiness. This quality of *muditā* is something very important we need to cultivate. A meditation master has put this very clearly. He said that we have a tendency to see what is wrong in ourselves, but we never look for what is right in ourselves.

The society might have harmful, destructive values but we should try to cultivate these virtues, these values that might be contrary to what is happening in society. This is why in the Buddha's teaching meditation is compared to going upstream, that it is not easy; most people just flow with the stream. So living in a society where these negative things are prominent, where they are given power, it is not easy to do this, it is difficult, but this is where we have to make an effort. This is where the practice is important. This is why a group of spiritual friends is important, and that at least we as a group are trying to practise these virtues, these qualities, even though in the country, in the society, something else is happening.

11
DEVELOPING LOVING-KINDNESS

A very important aspect of loving-kindness is learning to do kind things, learning to do compassionate things for others. When you develop more and more loving-kindness within yourselves, then naturally your actions, your speech, your words are related to this positive aspect of loving-kindness. And when you learn to be friendly to others, when you learn to be kind to others, when you learn to feel for others, this can also give lots of joy and happiness because when you see others being happy because of your own actions, this can bring lots of joy, lots of lightness to yourself.

But having loving-kindness is not about allowing others to exploit you, allowing others to do what they like to you. It is very important to learn that there are times when you have to assert yourselves, when you have to learn to be firm with others. In this connection I would like to relate a story that I like very much.

The story is about a cobra who was practising loving-kindness. This cobra was living in a forest practising loving-kindness, saying: "May all beings be well, may all beings be happy, may all beings be free of suffering."

There was an old woman living near the forest who could not see properly. She was collecting firewood, and when she saw the cobra she thought it was a rope, so she used it to tie the bundle of firewood she had collected. As the cobra was practising loving-kindness, it allowed the old woman to do this. The old woman carried the bundle of firewood home. Then, after some difficulty, the cobra escaped with lots of pain and with lots of wounds on its body.

Then the cobra went to meet his meditation master, and the cobra told the master: "See what has happened; I adopt the practice of loving-kindness, but see the wounds, see the pain that I'm experiencing in my body!" The master very calmly, very gently told the cobra: "You have not been practising loving-kindness, you have been practising foolish loving-kindness. You should have just shown by hissing that you are a snake!" So it is very important that in everyday life we also learn what the cobra should have learnt: that sometimes we have to hiss.

BENEFITS OF LOVING-KINDNESS

I would like to very briefly go over some of the benefits that are mentioned in a particular text about the meditation of loving-kindness. There are 11 benefits that are mentioned and some of them are extremely interesting. The first three are related to sleep: when you do meditation of loving-kindness you sleep peacefully, you wake up peacefully, and you do not see unpleasant dreams, nightmares. That is why in this retreat after the meditation of loving-kindness I say: May you sleep peacefully, and may you wake up peacefully. I hope you have been sleeping peacefully. If you have not been sleeping peacefully your meditation of loving-kindness has not been good. At least I am happy that you are waking up, because I have seen everyone this morning!

Another interesting benefit that is mentioned which is very logical—common sense—is that other human beings come to like you. Because it is natural when you like human beings, when you are friendly to others, they are bound to be friendly to you. So this is a very important tool to develop in relationships. If you want others to be friendly to you, you have to be friendly to them. When you have loving-kindness generally, this friendliness comes to you.

Another benefit is that non-humans also like you, not only human beings, even non-humans. Who can these non-humans be? Animals, angels, plants, flowers, gods—they say the gods protect you. It is funny that even gods protect you if you are full of loving-kindness. A good reason to practice loving-kindness! You get loving-kindness from human beings, you get loving-kindness from gods, you get loving-kindness even from animals.

Another benefit that is mentioned is that your face becomes serene, so you do not have any need for cosmetics. Loving-kindness is much cheaper! Then there is another benefit that is mentioned in relation to meditation. Your mind becomes calm quite naturally. This has a very important implication, that you can never experience calm by trying, by fighting, by resisting. That it has to come with more and more friendliness, it has to come with more and more gentleness. Then the mind becomes calm naturally.

I will mention one more benefit: it is said that when we die, we die unconfused, we die with awareness. Can anyone suggest a reason why it is important that we should die consciously, that we should die unconfused?

Retreatant: So we do not to go to hell!

Godwin: Well, that is a very negative way of putting it. Starting with a minus: hell! I think if we are unconfused, if there is awareness, we have a last chance to become enlightened. In fact there is a very interesting book, The Tibetan Book of the Dead, and that book explains that if we can die consciously—and there are some very interesting methods that are presented—then we have a really very good chance of becoming completely free at the time of dying.

What this book is presenting is what we are trying to do here: to recognise, to make friends with our monsters, our emotions. They can manifest themselves externally as very unpleasant demons. So if you recognise that they are projections of your own emotions, and if you have learned, as we are doing here, to understand them, to make friends with them, to create space for them, there is no problem with these figures that you are seeing. It is really recognising them for what they are. This is why I have been emphasising that we must learn to see things just as they are.

Another thing that is mentioned in this book is that our enlightened mind, our free mind, also manifests at this time. And if you can recognise that, and if you can just be with that, then that's it. That is why I am also suggesting to allow the positive, to see our free mind, the Buddha mind, to be aware of that, to know that. So all these things help us when we are living, all these things will help us when we are dying.

* * *

DISCUSSION

Those are some of the benefits that are mentioned in that book. Now let us see if we can include anything more, if we can add to this list from our own experience. Do you have any suggestions?

Retreatant: You will have no enemies, you will not have anyone whom you cannot get on with, and no hatred against another person.

Godwin: Very good one. In a way it is related to saying that human beings like you. To have enemies is when human beings don't like you. Anyway, as you say, to have no enemies is something very special. So what will happen is that you will have only friends and no enemies. What a wonderful way to live! Anything else?

Retreatant: It helps me to make clear decisions. That is, when there is hatred in my mind, then I always make the wrong decision because I would make a decision from my own point of view and not consider what others think.

Godwin: Very good. So when there is hatred, when there is anger, please don't take a decision because that decision will always be coming from a confused mind, not from a clear mind. Not only decisions but also words. I would suggest that if we get angry with someone then at that very moment we should just keep our mouths shut, because whatever we speak it doesn't come from a clear mind, so it can be confusing and can make matters worse. So the state of the mind in such a situation is very important.

On some occasions someone does something wrong and then we get angry and we try to correct that person with anger. I would suggest that to a great extent that type of reaction, trying to correct persons with anger, will not work. These are very important practical aspects of loving-kindness in everyday life. Anything more to add?

Retreatant: Before I learned about loving-kindness meditation, I easily got angry with others, but after I learned loving-kindness meditation I found the good thing about it is that the duration of anger gets shorter, and slowly the anger disappears altogether. Another benefit is that as you continue to train yourself you will find hating another person is really quite silly because it causes suffering for yourself. The more hatred you have, the more problems you create for yourself.

Godwin: Very good. Two good points. The first point is very important: how soon we recover from these emotions, hatred, anger, or whatever. I think you should not have as an ideal that you will not get angry, but if you need an ideal, the ideal should be how soon you recover from the anger.

There is a beautiful teaching in one of the Buddhist texts which gives three similes for three types of anger. The first type of anger is compared to letters written on stone which never change, never go away. The second type of anger is compared to letters written on sand, which will eventually disappear. The third type of anger is compared to letters written on water, which disappear immediately. Isn't that beautiful? That quickness: the anger is there and also it is already over.

And the second point is also very good, that it is silly, it is really foolish for us to hold on to anger and cause ourselves more suffering. I think this is compared to someone who is spitting in the wind, because when you spit in the wind it comes back on your own face. Anything else? It is very interesting that we can think creatively and add to the list of benefits like this.

Retreatant: It makes me feel warm, happy and pleasant all the time.

Godwin: That is true. This feeling of warmth is very important because now human beings are for various reasons becoming more and more cold. As I said at the nunnery, with mechanisation human beings are becoming more and more like machines, and one aspect of this is that they lack feelings. So having this warmth, having feelings for other people and for ourselves, is something very important, very beautiful.

Loving-kindness and Self-confidence

Another point I thought of which might be relevant to some of the people I have been meeting at the interviews is that loving-kindness can develop a sense of self-confidence. Can anyone see the connection between self-confidence and loving-kindness?

Retreatant: When you have loving-kindness you will do things quite easily that will help others, and you will think more of others and less of yourself. With this way of living, one can say one has no regrets at all in life, and when one can say that, this is self-confidence.

Godwin: I think another point about self-confidence is that we lose self-confidence when we consider ourselves as unsuccessful, worthless, useless, always failing. So it is a very negative self-image we have of ourselves, mostly as failures. With more and more loving-kindness, especially towards ourselves, we can see how it works: we can see our own potentialities and we can become more and more self-reliant, and this can give us a lot of self-confidence in the sense that we can handle whatever arises. It is not that difficulties will not arise; anger will arise, problems will arise, difficulties will arise, but you have the confidence if they arise: I know how to handle them, I know what to do.

Anyway, we can perhaps think of some more points. So it shows how important meditation on loving-kindness is, especially in everyday life, the changes that one can bring about in oneself, the transformation that one can bring about for oneself and, as I said, it is also bound to affect others around you.

Anger, Wounds and Forgiveness

Retreatant: The difficulty I have about practising loving-kindness is at the moment of anger itself. As you said, when I have a hating mind it is better not to make a decision and not even to say a word. My problem is that when I work in the office, when some of my staff do something wrong I immediately get angry and say something to them. Afterwards I know that I shouldn't have said it because I just add more suffering to the sufferings of the others and that's a mistake. I should have told them how to handle the mistake rather than raise my voice. I try very hard but it is always difficult to control myself at that moment of anger.

Godwin: Not only you, we can all relate to that experience. You have raised a very important, practical question. Sometimes I think you need to speak firmly to people with whom you work. Before I went to the meditation centre, I was a librarian. I tried to practise loving-kindness with the members of the staff there. It was not easy. People would come late, thinking: "He is practising loving-kindness, so we can get up an hour late. He is practising loving-kindness, so don't send in an application for leave, just stay at home!" I realised loving-kindness didn't work because some people understood only a different language. The only thing to do is to be very clear, that now I am going to be firm, speak to them very firmly. In doing that there is no wound made, there is no defilement created inside, there is just saying something that has to be said.

Anyway, the second part of the question has a very practical aspect. It is that when we get angry unexpectedly, what do we do? The first suggestion is: Don't be surprised! Because you are still practising. You are not enlightened. So don't be disappointed, don't feel guilty, don't get angry with yourself because you got angry. This is very important.

It can happen to meditators, especially when we take to meditation, that we form an image: "I am a meditator now. I am practising loving-kindness. This is how I should behave". It is good to have an ideal but an ideal is one thing, reality is another.

So at that moment when you have not been aware and you got angry, what you can do is just be with that anger without feeling bad: no need to give yourself a minus. Please realise that, it is very important.

But what has to be done is after you recover from that anger—maybe after five minutes, maybe after ten minutes, maybe after thirty minutes, it doesn't matter even if on the following day—when you have recovered then you reflect on that anger. And this kind of reflection has to be done in a very friendly, gentle way. Just to ask the question: What really happened to me? So you take your mind backwards and try to see the incident objectively, and also see the different aspects of that incident. Then our anger becomes the object of meditation. In this way our shortcomings, our failures, become learning experiences.

What is also important when we practise this way is that we don't have this fear to make mistakes; otherwise we become so concerned to do things perfectly, correctly, that this can generate such a lot of tension, such a lot of suffering. Please realise that this is not giving in to our shortcomings, but relating to them in an entirely different way, a more meaningful way, a more creative way, in a way that will reduce our suffering and enable us also to do what is necessary. Then you say to yourself: "Now let me see, next time I face such a situation how will I behave?" And just wait and see. So you are waiting for such opportunities to see how your behaviour is. To put it in another way, although you have got angry there is no wound. Then we come to a state where, when we have got angry, there is less suffering as a result, and I think this is a very important state.

Retreatant: You said there might have been things done wrongly in the past where we did not forgive others and did not forgive ourselves, and usually we suppress these things in our heart. At this moment, how do I know whether I have suppressed these things in the past and need to bring them out to heal them?

Godwin: Very good. Let's take a practical situation where a wound has been created in relation to what you have done to another person; you have acted incorrectly and then you suffer from guilt. The first point is to realise how the wound was created in the first place. So when you enquire into that question you realise the wound has been created by your idea: This is how I should have behaved. You realise the problem is with your model of how you should behave. It is helpful to understand this because this can help us to heal the wound. This is the first point.

The second point is to realise that we are still human, we are still imperfect, so therefore, as I have been saying very often, we need to learn to forgive our humanness, to forgive our imperfections.

Another suggestion is to realise that these things happened in the past. I cannot change the past, so why I am holding onto something that has happened in the past?

The last point—I hope I can communicate this—is that we carry the wounds in our memory. And as they are related to memories, the more we try to forget them the more they come. We have no control over our memory. The control we have is not in relation to the memory itself but how we respond to the memory. This is where meditation comes in. This is where we can work with it in practical terms. So when the memory comes in relation to what you have done, what you can observe is your reaction to the memory: guilt.

Now this is where awareness is relevant: with awareness we learn that there is guilt, and as we have also been practising, we learn to say okay to that guilt, we learn to feel friendly with that guilt, just to allow that guilt. Then after some time you might remember that incident again and then again guilt will come, so again we create space for that guilt to be there. It can also be interesting sometimes to deliberately and consciously bring the memory up and see how we are relating to it. Then one day you have the experience, the memory comes, but there is no guilt, and when that happens it shows that the wound is healed. Then the memory might come but the corresponding emotion will not be there. We might even deliberately and consciously bring up the memory and the corresponding emotion will not be there.

One last suggestion is to realise that holding onto such wounds is something very self-destructive. So these are ways and means of healing such wounds. Whether it is guilt, whether it is grief, whether it is hatred, the tools are the same.

Retreatant: Today I deliberately brought some memories up to see if there are wounds or not but there was no reaction. Could it be a delusion? Would such a thing happen?

Godwin: This shows they have been healed. So no need to feel worried, thinking: I don't have wounds, or, why don't I have wounds? You can give yourself a plus because most people still have wounds. Then just to say: I don't have wounds, it's good.

I think on one occasion I said to those who do not have wounds, please send loving-kindness to those who are trying to heal their wounds, because some people are really struggling with wounds. I know it is so strong in them, so deep in them, that it takes a lot for them to heal these memories. I know this by experience, through working with meditators.

Retreatant: You taught us the practice of loving-kindness and how we should be friendly with ourselves and others and how we should reflect on wounds that we have and forgive others. But how do we know we are really being sincere in forgiving ourselves and in forgiving others?

Godwin: Very good question. I will give a practical example. Supposing you have a wound in relation to what you have done to another: guilt. So before healing the wound, whenever a thought came in relation to your action you would suffer from guilt. Now the wound will be healed when the memory comes and on reflection there is no guilt. In the same way, someone has been very unfriendly and unkind to you and whenever the memory comes in relation to his or her action you feel hatred, you feel anger, you feel ill-will. The wound is healed when the memory comes about that person but no hatred, no ill-will comes.

I'm happy you reminded us of wounds. Tomorrow is the last full day you have for healing wounds, so I would like to suggest you try to heal them and leave all the wounds here when you go from here.

✎ **Retreatant:** About others wounds: for example, one of my male friends thinks I wounded him but this is not so, I did nothing wrong. How can I help him to get rid of the wound?

❈ **Godwin:** So other people have wounds in relation to our behaviour. We might try to heal their wounds by trying to explain to them; or if you have really created the wound, say sorry to them, and then try to help them to heal their wound. You can always try. Sometimes we find it difficult, so they, too, may find it difficult to heal them. But what is important is for you not to suffer as a result of that, because what can you do about it? You have done your best, and then the other person doesn't want to heal that wound. So let us not create a wound in our own mind in relation to their wound.

✎ **Retreatant:** Are love and hate the same thing?

❈ **Godwin:** Can you give us some examples? I am a simple man. I like practical examples.

✎ **Retreatant:** You mentioned that if our wound is hatred we can deliberately bring it up and look at the hatred, and if we have no reaction to it that means the wound is healed. But what about love: can we dig up situations where we have loved others, and then see if we have any emotion when we dig out this memory of love? For instance, not only after a parting of ways, but if for some reason you have sacrificed yourself for his or her good there can be deep emotions when these memories are dug out. Should they be treated in the same way as we deal with anger?

❈ **Godwin:** When you remember such things, or when you can deliberately and consciously bring them up without any unpleasant emotions, what you will be having is pleasant emotions. You can feel happy about what you have done for another person.

I would suggest that it is important for us also sometimes to think of the good things we have done. This can give us lots of joy, lots of happiness, lots of lightness, and it will also be an incentive to do more and more such actions of love. In Sri Lanka we used to have a custom—now it is no longer there—to keep what is called a book of merits. The idea is that you note down the good things you have done, the skilful things you have done, and at the time you are dying someone reads from the book. Because usually we give more power, more energy to our mistakes, and I think this is very important. In fact it is mentioned in the Dhamma, to deliberately and consciously acknowledge our goodness, so when these memories come up you should acknowledge those positive emotions.

Working with Wounds from Childhood

- **Retreatant:** What can I do about childhood wounds?

- **Godwin:** You are raising a very important question. I did not speak about childhood wounds, because I knew it would come up. Because I have been encountering this with many meditators that I have been meeting. So I will try to give you a full reply because I feel this is extremely important.

It might interest you that in Sri Lanka I do not meet people who speak to me about childhood wounds. This was fascinating for me when I was meeting Westerners. They invariably speak about their childhood wounds in the context of meditation. In the beginning I told them just to be aware, forgiving. Then I realised it was not working because these wounds are really deep.

I will share with you the ways and means I have discovered within my own limitations. Earlier when someone had a childhood wound that related to their parents, I told them, in the beginning, just to forgive them, have loving-kindness towards them. They got very angry when I spoke of forgiveness. Because of the anger I stopped doing it. Now one other thing I suggest to them is this. The meditation centre in Sri Lanka is quite big and there is a forest around it, so I tell them to go somewhere and bring out the anger about their mother and father—I would not tell my Sri Lankan friends about this. I do it very secretly! I tell them to bring up the anger, and when they are able to do so, to a full extent, then I would make the suggestion how it is possible just to forgive them.

Sometimes I use some principles of a psychotherapy which I learned originally from another meditation teacher. So, in a meditative state of mind, with some calmness and clarity, some space, I get people to reflect on three questions. The questions are: What are the good things you have done for your parents? What are the good things they have done for you? What are the difficulties you have created for your parents? I have heard some very interesting answers. Sometimes when they reflect on these three questions certain memories, certain things they have forgotten, come up.

It is fascinating that we have such a selective memory. With this selective memory we are holding on to only the minuses, but with this simple practical exercise you bring up the plusses in your parents. And then you realise that you have also created some difficulties for your parents. Then the meditators come to me and say: "Now I feel guilty!" Then I know the meditation has worked. So this is one thing I try to do in working with childhood problems. Another thing I try to emphasise is: do you realise that your parents are only human? Do you realise that they have not been capable of behaving in another way? Don't you realise that you may be the victim of someone who is another victim?

As I mention this, I will share with you a very moving story I heard from a woman that I was working with. She had had the most terrible childhood. Her mother was beating her physically and mentally, and, hearing some other things she described, I was horrified. And it naturally affected her substantially. And of course she carried a big wound in her mind because of her mother. And she had lost contact with her completely. After many, many years when this woman was in her 50's or 60's she made inquiries about her mother. Then she heard that she was in a home for old people. So she found out where she was and she went to visit her there, and when she met the mother, she hugged her and with all her heart she said: "I love you, Mother." The mother was crying, not saying anything. Then this woman asked:

"Why can't you say that you love me?" The mother replied: "How can I say I love you? I have never known what love is." When she heard those words, the wounds she had been carrying for many, many years healed then and there. So what do we know about our parents? It is easy to give them minuses.

Another thing I try to tell the meditators I meet is that anything might have happened in childhood, anything might have happened at birth. Actually it is interesting to see the Western models regarding this, and how they change. With Freud it was childhood experiences, after Freud it was birth trauma and now I hear it is reincarnation therapy.

Then you start digging and digging for childhood experiences and even that is not enough now. You have to start digging down to what happened at birth, and that is still not enough. You have to start digging for what has happened in previous lives. They have a compulsion to go deeper and deeper. I met such a reincarnation therapist in Germany during my previous visit, he had written a book about it, and very seriously he was telling me: One life is not enough, you have to go back at least 3 lives!

So I tell people: Anything might have happened in previous lives, anything might have happened at birth, anything might have happened in childhood, what are you doing about it now? It is very easy to blame previous lives, it is very easy to blame what has happened at birth, it is very easy to blame your parents. But here and now do you take responsibility?

The model that is presented in meditation is: be in the present and whatever has to come naturally—please realise this—whatever has to come naturally from the past, with gentleness let it come. This is the importance of silence, one aspect of silence.

Sometimes the need to talk is really to prevent certain things from coming up. In some of these intensive retreats people have shared with me some very deep memories coming up from the past, just popping up. Another thing is, I will be presenting a meditation technique where the whole emphasis is to allow things to arise. So once your mind is calm, spacious, stable—this is very important—then you can allow anything to arise in relation to thoughts, any emotions to arise, any sensation to arise. And how do we prevent these things from arising? It is again by giving a minus, controlling, pushing them away. It is extremely important just to learn to allow them without a minus, without controlling. Then if they have to come, if there is a need for them to come, they will emerge. And this is the importance again of awareness: when they arise, can you just be aware of them? And if there are strong emotions, can you just be with these emotions?

So this is what I try to suggest when I meet meditators who have childhood problems.

Forgiving Oneself and Forgiving Others

I would like to ask a question, and I ask this whenever I visit a foreign country. Which is easier to do: to forgive oneself or to forgive others? Please reflect on this and give an answer from your heart.

- **Retreatant:** It's not easy to forgive oneself.
- **Godwin:** Does everyone agree?
- **Retreatant:** No.

(By show of hands, the retreatants indicated whether they considered it easier to forgive themselves or whether they considered it easier to forgive others).

- **Godwin:** Thank you. What does this indicate? It indicates that those who find it difficult to forgive themselves, are very hard on themselves. Thus they are too stonehearted towards themselves saying: I don't deserve to be forgiven. And then those who find it difficult to forgive others, they are being very hard on others. So you see the importance of developing softness, you realise the importance of being gentle, the importance of feeling tender to oneself and to others. When you develop these qualities, naturally you can forgive yourself and you can forgive others.

As I said, what we have to learn, and I think it is extremely important, is to accept our humanness, to accept that we are imperfect human beings, that we still have shortcomings. In the same way we have to realise that we are living in a world where other people are imperfect, where other people are still only human, so we're bound to see the shortcomings, human frailties, arising in others and in ourselves.

According to the Buddha's teaching there is greed, there is hatred, there is delusion both in us and in other people. So because of greed, hatred, and delusion, we all have shortcomings and make mistakes. Only someone who is completely enlightened will not have these shortcomings; but as long as we are not enlightened we are still only human, we are imperfect.

I feel that it is extremely important to realise this, to accept this and learn to forgive ourselves and to forgive others. Then when you can see things in these terms, as I said, you will be able to forgive yourself and forgive others.

Retreatant: You said we should learn to love ourselves as a friend, but when we see the bad thoughts or bad desires in us how can we love this friend when this friend is so bad? Isn't that like covering up for ourselves in a way?

Godwin: Very good question. We will take a couple of practical examples. Take the example of anger, when we get angry, what happens? We are angry about our anger. We start sometimes hating ourselves because we are getting angry, and then we suffer from guilt because we have got angry. Because of this anger and because you are relating to it in this way you can suffer for days.

Now in using loving-kindness you relate to the anger in an entirely different way. Rather than beating yourself, rather than giving yourself a minus, rather than suffering and feeling guilty, in a very friendly, gentle way, as I have been saying so often, you'll find out: How did I get angry?

Then we can learn from that anger, we can use that anger for our spiritual growth. This is what I mean by being friendly. The way I'm suggesting helps us to work with the anger in an entirely different way rather than giving in to it. It's not really pampering ourselves, but it is learning to work with the anger in a different way, in a more effective way, rather than suffering too much as a result of that anger.

And another point is, when you are friendly to yourself and when you are open to yourself you will also realise when you're not angry, which is also very important. So then we come to a stage that when we are angry we know what to do with the anger, and when we are not angry we know we are not angry.

Retreatant: Learning to practise forgiveness is easier to say than to do, especially when it comes to people who are close to you like parents, very good friends, brothers and sisters. It is very difficult to forgive them. When it comes to friends who are not so close to you, not so friendly, then it's easier to forgive them. What can we do?

Godwin: Very interesting question, which I think all of us can relate to. It is interesting actually to reflect why people to whom we are close can create such wounds. The simple reason is that because they are close to us, maybe friends or relations, then we have an image, an expectation about how they should behave.

A good simile to understand this is that first we put them on a pedestal by saying he's my best friend. Then my best friend should behave in a certain way. Or we think: "She's my mother and therefore she should behave in this way." So you see the demands we are making on people because they are close to us and, poor people, they fall from the pedestal that we have put them on. And when they fall from the pedestal we don't realise that we are the persons who put them on the pedestal in the first place, and we get disappointed, we suffer. And a person can carry these wounds throughout their life.

So you should really see what happens to you because of the ideas you have about how others should behave. To put the same thing another way, we forget that they are also human.

Retreatant: Do you mean we should not have any expectations of others, or should we not be attached to people?

❀ **Godwin:** I think it is natural that we have expectations, but what we forget is how far are our expectations realistic? How far are you prepared to meet up with your expectations about yourself? How far can others meet up with your expectations about them? How realistic are your expectations? This is what one has to be clear about.

I know some people who are very idealistic: very idealistic about themselves, very idealistic about others, and so they live in a very idealistic world. This idealistic world that they have created is one thing and what they are experiencing is another thing. So as long as we hold onto this idealistic world, hold onto this perfect world, we are bound to create wounds in relation to our own behaviour and in relation to the behaviour of others.

According to the Buddha, until and unless we are enlightened we are all crazy. Crazy in the sense that we can't see things as they are. The problem with us is we take this crazy world seriously. And also I would like to give a reminder of a very interesting saying in Tibetan Buddhism: Enlightened people behave like ordinary people, while ordinary people try to behave like enlightened people!

LOVING-KINDNESS AND SELF-IMAGE

☙ **Retreatant:** You said earlier that we should not create an image about ourselves. But when we practise meditation of loving-kindness we create an image of ourselves that we are full of loving-kindness, so are the two things contradictory?

❀ **Godwin:** Very good question, very good question. So in a way we need to have images, even to have expectations. What is important for us to realise is in what ways we are using them destructively. Then if we don't have these qualities in us, if instead of loving-kindness we have hatred, hatred towards ourselves, hatred towards others, then it is very important to bring about a shift within ourselves by learning to be our best friend, learning to be a friend to others. In this way it is no harm having an image: "I want to be a person who is friendly and tries to practise". Or you can still practise without an image but just develop these qualities and allow your behaviour to emerge from that.

So one can really practise at two levels: if you like to have an image, you can have it, but otherwise you can just practise without an image and allow your behaviour to arise from whatever spiritual qualities you have developed. What is important is to see whether that image corresponds to reality. This is what we have to work with. Images create problems sometimes if the images are unrealistic. When you have an image of how things should be and then what happens in reality is another thing, this is how suffering is created. So there are different aspects to this question. I'm very happy that good questions are being asked.

12
A SPIRITUAL APPROACH TO FRIENDSHIP

What I will try to do is to present the solution found in the Dhamma for problems arising in relationships. And there is a beautiful phrase that is used in this connection. Even in Pali the words sound very nice: *kalyana-mitta*, which means a spiritual friend or a noble friend. I will try to present some problems, difficulties, that human beings experience in relationships which I have been hearing about so often and then see how one can work with these problems and build up real spiritual friendships where we can really grow together.

So you begin with yourself. How do you relate to yourself? I have been emphasising this aspect very much, where you learn to be your own best friend. If you can really make that connection with yourself then you see relationships in a different way. Creating more suffering for oneself and more suffering for others may become less, or may not be there at all. This is the first point in a spiritual relationship.

DIFFICULTIES IN RELATIONSHIPS

I think another situation which human beings have to face in relating to other human beings is to do with what they consider the shortcomings of others. What do you do when you see someone behaving in a way which you think they should not?

Retreatant: Give a big minus.

Godwin: We start with a very, very big minus, that is true. And anything else? Do we stop with a minus?

Retreatant: Sometimes we make the minus bigger. There is a German saying: Making an elephant out of a fly.

❋ **Godwin:** Very good point. So you need only to give a very small minus, but then you make it very big. And some people are very creative. They can speak for the whole morning or the whole night about this small minus. And they speak as if they do not have any minuses themselves! This is another very interesting phenomenon. They speak from a standpoint of perfection. They forget that they are capable of behaving in the same way.

These are things that one has to realise. And maybe another thing which we do is, we do not stop at a big minus, but then we get really angry, we try to point out the mistake while being very angry with the person. And then because we are angry and are showing it, with this anger we are hurting the other person. And then what does the other person do?

☙ **Retreatant:** He gets angry also.

❋ **Godwin:** He also gets angry. Naturally, you get angry and you hurt the other person and the other person tries to return a bigger hurt. Then it becomes a competition, to see who can be most hurtful! And if the other person is not getting angry, how would you respond to that?

☙ **Retreatant:** You would complain: You do not even get angry!

❋ **Godwin:** Exactly. Sometimes such people are meditators also: after all we are still only human. So aren't relationships very interesting? Isn't it really valuable to learn from such situations?

In a spiritual relationship, when you see someone doing something wrong, do you say: May you be well, may you be happy, may you be peaceful? Do you say: These minuses are only concepts, I do not use minuses? What will a spiritual friend do in such a situation? He will speak with the other person, want him to grow. He will engage in kind of a dialogue, for a spiritual friend would try to get the other person to understand his behaviour. Because sometimes we only *assume* that the other person understands why he is behaving in this way. So it is something very useful to get that person to understand or reflect about his behaviour. And then the spiritual friend does something very creative also. When the other person does not do anything wrong, the spiritual friend points that out too! It is extremely destructive to point out only the minuses, to point out only when the other person does something wrong. It is extremely important to tell the other person when the other person is doing something good, something skilful, something wholesome. This is a quality we need to cultivate. The other quality you do not have to cultivate, it is there naturally!

It needs some effort to see these positive qualities and to say this with your whole heart and to really show your deep appreciation for these things, and this can be something very touching. There can be a beautiful communication when such a thing happens. Then that spiritual friend does the same thing to you. It is sharing with each other, not taking up a position: I am better, or I am superior to you. But really sharing together, learning together, growing together.

And sometimes it is also important to know when it is necessary to be assertive. So you should know when to be gentle and when to be assertive. I will share with you an experience of what a woman in Sri Lanka told me about in this connection. This was when I was in a very remote village speaking to a group of meditators. And one of the women shared this experience with the group: She said that her husband would come home drunk and he would break the pots, the plates, the cups and so on. She tried so many things, practising loving-kindness, speaking to him in a very kind, gentle way when he was sober. She spoke to his other friends, and through the friends she tried to influence him. She would collect all that he had broken and keep it in a place where he could see it. All these tools did not work. At last one day when he came home drunk she said: "If you break one plate, I will break ten!" That was the end of his breaking plates! So, as a spiritual friend, you have to use these methods in a skilful way and not always simply be passive. Some people understand only this language. This is another point to remember.

Another thing is when you realise that the other person is closed. I have been hearing this very often since coming here [in Germany]. And I have also noticed the gesture that they use here. Now, I know even Sri Lankans would say: "My friend is moody, he does not speak," but they do not use this gesture. So I am very curious to know, please tell me, what this gesture really means.

Retreatant: It means there is a shutter coming down.

Godwin: Some tell me: When I am open, his shutter comes down. And when he is open, my shutter comes down! Is that correct? As a spiritual friend, what do you do with the shutters? Very practical question. Any suggestions? Any solutions?

Retreatant: Let the person be in peace.

Godwin: Leave the person with closed shutters in peace. May you be peaceful!

Retreatant: You can wait for their opening up.

Godwin: We can wait until the shutters open.

Retreatant: Or you can stop playing the emotional tango for a while, and after a while you try again. Perhaps if you are lucky it opens.

Godwin: In a creative relationship maybe it might be helpful to explore all this, because it is possible that the person really does not know under what circumstances it happens. He or she may not have control over it. So this is where if two people have a connection, have a concern for each other, what is beautiful is if they can explore these things, discuss these things, have a Dhamma discussion. And then see how they can slowly, slowly, try to see whether the shutter can open. Sometimes it is very useful to get feedback because the one who is doing this may not realise under what circumstances it happens, what triggers off this situation. So it is really very helpful, this kind of exploration together. Then the person knows: When my shutter goes down, my friend is not hurt by this, my friend understands me.

I feel if you can have this kind of concern and care—I do not know whether I should make this grand statement—whatever problems may arise it may be possible to work them out in some way together, rather than trying to work them out alone by yourself. I mean it is something very, very supportive to find someone else helping you, and to be helping each other like this.

Handling of Difficulties in Relationships

I think another challenge we have, again a skill to learn, something to cultivate, is that when there are differences to try to really understand the other person from his or her position. Here again, you become so fixed with your own conclusions, your own ideas about things, your own assumptions, your own idealism or whatever, that it is extremely difficult to forget all that for a moment and see the other person from his or her position.

This is a very interesting practice. It is not easy, but just to try to forget your own world and try to understand the world of the other person. It is like playing with a child. If you want to learn to play with a child, you have to forget your own world, and enter into their world—and it is something really beautiful to get into the world of the child. Then you can communicate with the child, you can communicate with the other individual in this way. Otherwise naturally the two worlds clash and there cannot be any communication. This is another skill, so you see in a spiritual relationship how it allows us to develop these very important skills, these very important spiritual qualities.

What are the other challenges we have? I think another challenge we all have is that we have become so dependent on what others think of us. It is a great need we have, a need for plusses from other people. I'd like to mention that it can be a very strong need. But here again, if you are serious in growing up you have to work with this dependency because otherwise it can become a problem where you are all the time trying to please others, all the time trying to get plusses from others. And then if you are not getting plusses from others you think you are not trying enough and then you try even harder and it can become really a vicious circle. What is the basis of this need to become so dependent on the plusses of others?

Retreatant: Emotional insecurity, and lack of self-acceptance.

Godwin: Here again it means that it depends on how you relate to yourself. So you see how important it is to examine how you relate to yourself, which is why I emphasise this ability to see yourself as your own best friend and really become self-contained within yourself.

Sometimes I like to use this metaphor of toys. Although we are grown up we still need these external toys. Sometimes we can be changing one toy for another and then not getting satisfied with that toy. It is a case of just continuing to change toys and still not really being content, not really being self-contained. This is one of the greatest challenges we have. This is why I have been encouraging you to spend some time alone and see when being alone, do you feel lonely, do you feel bored with yourself? See how far you can learn to be your own best friend in that situation. If that connection can be made then you become your own toy. And when you can see yourself as your toy you can find yourself very amusing, entertaining, interesting. You have everything within yourself.

Then something beautiful happens. When you are alone you can play with the toy and when you are with others you can enjoy others. This is another challenge we have in relationships, again using that to grow spiritually. Then, whether you get plusses or minuses from others, whether you get praise or disapproval from others, you become self-contained within yourself.

Dealing with Difficult People

What are the other challenges we have, problems we have, difficulties we have in relating to human beings? Sometimes, for different reasons, one may be in a position of having to work with or to relate to a person who can be extremely unreasonable, authoritative and so on. I have been hearing from meditators that sometimes you have such a boss in the places where you are working. He or she does not believe in spiritual relationships. He is a very ruthless boss, he or she wants things done in his or her own way.

How does one work with such a person? Sometimes such a boss may not only be at work, there might be such a boss at home also. Perhaps your neighbour can become such a person. How do we work with these real challenges that we have in relationships? Do you leave the job, do you leave the house? Do you find another house because the neighbour is the boss?

Retreatant: I think the best way is to try to understand the other person, try to have a little talk with the neighbour, understand what happened in his life, why he is the way he is.

Godwin: Anything else?

Retreatant: Try to send the boss loving-kindness.

Godwin: Try to send the boss loving-kindness: "May the boss be well, may he be more peaceful, may he not create suffering for me!" What I would like to suggest is something entirely different: that you start experimenting, exploring, using the boss as your most valuable teacher. Like when inviting the monsters you say: "Now today I hope my boss will show his or her power. Because this morning I had a very good meditation, I have a lot of space in the mind. I have a lot of clarity, I did loving-kindness meditation this morning, so let me see what will happen with the boss." Then you are prepared.

Some days the meditator is successful, the boss did everything possible but there was no problem. You should give yourself a big plus, and feel grateful to the boss. But as we are still human, there are some days when loving-kindness meditation did not work, morning meditation did not work, and then there is hurt, disappointment, and wounds. Then, what do you do? Do you give up meditation?

Retreatant: Not go to the office.

Godwin: Isn't it interesting: one failure, one time you fail and that is it. So what you can do, and this is a very important practice, when we have failed and when we have recovered from that, try to reflect on it and make that the object of meditation. This has to be done only when you have recovered from the wound that has been created. And it has to be done in a friendly, gentle and kind way. Not to have a kind of stick: "Now what happened? Why didn't my meditation work? That shouldn't have happened," and so on. Because then there is more hatred, more guilt, more feeling worthless.

Now this is the beauty of having a spiritual friendship with oneself. So like having a dialogue with another spiritual friend you have this friendly dialogue with yourself: "What really happened to you, my dear? At what point did the monster arise? How many monsters came?" Here you have to be very truthful and honest, to acknowledge that this and that happened. But there's no need to give a big minus, just acknowledge it, realise it, that that is what happened.

Or perhaps you can even give yourself a big plus: "It is OK, I am still trying, I am still human, I am still imperfect, but it is nice that I am still continuing on with my practice—wonderful!" You go the next day, go the next week, see what will happen then. Then you come to a state that whether you are successful or whether you have failed makes no difference, because in both situations they can become objects of meditation. Isn't that an interesting way to live? Isn't that a beautiful way to live? Learning from our failures, learning from our mistakes.

Here again, Thich Nhat Hanh says something very beautiful. He says: Compost is something that is dirty, but you can use the compost to grow flowers. So this is our compost. Learning to use the compost to grow, to grow spiritually. What is the problem? And all that is due to the very good teacher.

Getting to Know Our Boundaries

☙ **Retreatant:** If we do what you tell us to, do we have to take everything as a teacher? For example, when a husband comes home and beats his wife, should we take him as a teacher? Also if I have to go to work with a very unpleasant boss and I have to go there for 40 or 50 years, I think it is better to look for another job.

❀ **Godwin:** Or in the meantime the boss may die within these 40 to 50 years! Anyway, that important question brings up the point that we must know our boundaries. Here is another challenge in relationships, in spiritual life: to know our boundaries. Talking of boundaries, I have a very interesting relationship with this little guru here, this little child [Godwin indicates a young child in the room]: we are slowly, slowly becoming friends. When I give him something he takes it, when I smile, sometimes he smiles. When I play, sometimes he will also try to play. But he knows his boundaries very, very well. I tried to carry him twice, but he pushed me away: just be friends at a distance. This is how a child of that age indicates its boundaries. When I touch his body to carry him—body language!

This is real communication! So I just took this as an example of how we should be very clear about our boundaries. Like the little guru saying no. Sometimes you must also say: Now it is enough. Enough with the boss, enough with whoever it is.

You can make a choice: Do I let it pass or do I give in to it? Or do I act like the snake, the cobra? Sometimes in relationships we need to be like the cobra in the story I mentioned before when the teacher told the cobra: "Sometimes you have to hiss!"

Yes, anything else?

Retreatant: Yes, I would say that if we are in a relationship we also have to see what is the real way to help the other person. If I come back to the example with the woman and her husband beating her—if she leaves the husband then she gives him a chance to see what was happening, what he has been doing.

Godwin: This is very, very important, this reflection. This is why I suggested that sometimes you can do these reflections together, the two people who are involved. Or, if you are unable to do that, to really reflect on it yourself. This is why I have been encouraging this practice of reflection.

Retreatant: The husband comes home and takes it out on the wife, and the wife takes it out on the children, that is possible.

Godwin: And the children take it out on the dog! Anyway, I have been presenting some areas for you to reflect on. So now is the time to ask questions. Please ask questions about important issues in relationships, practical questions, relate some practical situations.

Discussing Difficulties Together

✧ **Retreatant:** What if you have the impression that your partner was overwhelmed for a while with her emotions, and did not act for a while in a normal way, like she was quite out of control, leaving you and going to another partner? And then after some time she recognises that she was overwhelmed by her emotions. What should one do if after some time this person wants to come back?

✺ **Godwin:** I have not thought of such a situation before, but let us reflect. Suppose you are a meditator and then such a thing happens, how does one deal with such a situation? I think you must try to reflect on what is happening in you. Now, this kind of reflection has to be done when there is space, when there is some clarity, when one can see the situation very, very clearly, as far as possible. Now the first question to reflect on is: why did she leave me in the first place? Was there anything that I was doing that resulted in this? And as I said earlier, trying to see it from her point of view—that is very, very important.

So as I said, to have that kind of space, to see it from her position, one has to have a lot of understanding. And when that type of reflection is practised I am sure there will be questions, doubts that will arise in your mind. When the person has come back, can we have an honest dialogue with her?

Now here in this dialogue, as a meditator it does not mean that you have to always be passive and say: It is wonderful that you have come back! But in this dialogue one has to question her, find out why she did it, under what circumstances she did it, so this kind of dialogue gives her an opportunity to really reflect on her own behaviour. If, in this kind of dialogue, reflection can take place it is something very, very helpful, something very creative, where two individuals are really understanding, trying to understand their behaviour. And, through that, a connection may be made, it depends on the situation. You may be in a state to reflect: Can I heal my wound in this situation? And if you are unable to heal the wound, maybe you should tell her honestly: "This is my situation."

13
Problems of Everyday Life

Retreatant: How can I distinguish between being able to change things, and when I have to accept something as it is?

Godwin: Very good question! You should be clear what you can change and you should be clear what cannot be changed. And one area where change is possible is ourselves. Beginning from there we can also see what can be changed outside. And to be realistic as far as possible as to what cannot be changed. We have a saying displayed in this connection at the Nilambe Meditation Centre: "May I have the courage to change what can be changed, the patience to bear what cannot be changed, and the wisdom to know the difference between the two". Any other questions?

Retreatant: How can I change without being under pressure?

Godwin: You are quite right to ask this. I meet many people who are putting pressure on themselves to change. When I meet them I realise they are only putting pressure on, and not really changing themselves. I was telling one of the meditators, I have been meeting what I call 'casualties of meditation', who have been putting the pressure on to change themselves. Casualties: they have some problem in the mind, some problem in the body, but really they are quite okay, and then the pressure to change arises and straightaway some complication develops in the mind or the body. So now I am wondering if meditation is really helping these people. Because non-meditators are much happier. I am really seriously thinking about this question, about what people are doing to themselves in the name of meditation.

I will give a simple example. Close to the Nilambe Meditation Centre there is a town called Kandy. In Kandy for people who are not meditating, noise is no problem, crowds are no problem for them, seeing nice food is no problem for them. But when Nilambe meditators come to Kandy, they cannot relate to the noise, they cannot relate to the crowds, they have a problem with ice cream! Do you know what they do? They run back to the Centre! So that was good for the Centre. But I thought seriously, what am I doing here? Am I producing meditators who are worse off than non-meditators?

This is why I emphasise such a lot about working with our monsters, about making friends as far as possible with things. Because, like here, Nilambe is an ideal place for the monsters to go to sleep. So I try not to allow that situation to arise. In a way there are sometimes more challenges there than there are here. Especially when a group of Sri Lankans come. They cannot stop talking! I know some meditators hate it when they hear a Sri Lankan group is coming. The room that they have been holding on to as 'their' room, they suddenly find two Sri Lankans sharing 'their' room. And I hope the newcomers would start snoring in the night! I see that as the practice. Having calm experiences, having very pleasant experiences—when you leave Nilambe, and you go to Kandy, all that is gone. So this is why I do not encourage people to go into deep states of concentration.

Buddhist monks come to the Centre for meditation and when they come, sometimes I encourage them to go into deep states of samādhi, because in the type of life that they lead they can function in that situation. But for lay people like you who have to have relationships, who have to work with computers, who have to live in big towns, where you hear only telephones, trams, trucks, busses, and so on it doesn't work. One can have deep experiences in Nilambe then return to your homes and work—and all of it is gone straightaway. But it is different if, while people are in Nilambe, they can work with emotions, they can work with monsters, if they can really learn to work with them—then when they are in big towns, when these things arise they are not taken by surprise. This is why I offer many tools. This is why I am encouraging you to use the tools here. So when you learn to use the tools here, when you go back, when these monsters come, you can see how far you can apply them.

Pressure to be Perfect

When I started to speak the question was not so relevant to what I am now saying, so how easily I can go on to other things! I have to be aware of my speech. Anyway I was trying to respond to the point he made, about how we pressurise ourselves to change ourselves. This is why I have been emphasising as a first step: Please accept yourself as you are, not as you should be, or as you must be. This is extremely important. Otherwise all the time we want to be different from what we are. All the time we are pushing ourselves, pressurising ourselves to be different from what we are. One person used the word ego. We are trying to get rid of the ego, but in this process we are creating a bigger ego! This is why I am speaking about finding a way of practising without pressurising yourself. But please realise this does not mean giving in to these things.

As I was telling someone today, one has to find a spiritual life, a meditation practice, which suits the culture here. In the culture here you have to pressurise yourself to do well in life. You have to pressurise yourself to succeed in this culture. And in this culture you are pressurised to act perfectly. The model of perfection is imposed on you by the culture here. Do you see the connection? When such people take to meditation, they want to be a perfect meditator. As I said, they start pressurising themselves and demanding from themselves: I should be like this, I should be like that. And guilt is a great problem here. Then they start feeling guilty because they are not making any progress in the spiritual practice.

So poor meditators! They started by wanting to work on suffering. Now they are having more suffering because of meditation! And then they start pressurising more. I am really deeply touched when I meet such people. Because they are very sincere, genuine, highly motivated people. I think this is something for us to reflect on.

Retreatant: How can I handle the tools without putting pressure on myself to find the right one each time?

Godwin: I like such questions, it shows the confused way I have been teaching! I would like to meet you individually, but still I will say some general things about the question. The first point is why do I offer so many tools? It's because I know there are different sorts of people. There are different people and they are in different situations. In a retreat like this there are complete newcomers and there are some who have practised for many, many years. This is why I really encourage people to see me personally, because what I try to do is to relate to people individually. And that is why I offer many techniques, and that is why I am encouraging you to experiment, to explore and find out what is most helpful to you in the place you are at.

GIVING PLUSSES AND MINUSES

I would like to say something about this plus and minus business. In this culture I meet many people who are used to giving themselves minuses. That is why when I spoke about meditation of loving-kindness, I mentioned that you have to develop loving-kindness towards yourselves. You have to learn to see more and more plusses in yourself. It is extremely important, as I have been often saying, that we should learn to feel happy about what we are doing. We should feel grateful for what we are trying to do. With more and more plusses you really experience more joy, more lightness and so on. Once rid of the mechanism of giving minuses you experience these plusses, you experience this joy, this lightness, this happiness, and gratitude.

Actually this state itself is wonderful. But if you would like to go further you have to see that these positive experiences, that these plusses are also *anicca*, that they are also impermanent. And they are also, in a way, empty. That is, they are empty of any owner as I tried to indicate this morning. And then you go beyond plus and minus; you realise that both are concepts. When you realise that, you can use them as concepts when you want to, but you're fully realising the nature of concepts.

But let us forget about this third level and let us be more concerned about the second where we can have more loving-kindness, more friendliness, more gratitude, more joy, more lightness. That is good enough. But while you are experiencing them, I would also like you to work with unpleasant monsters, negative emotions, so that in everyday life you are really ready for them when they arise.

Now I would like to say something about being a little more positive. There is a very positive effect in writing down everyday the good things which happen throughout the day. About this I would like to make a brief comment. When I meet meditators in Nilambe I do a very interesting exercise in this connection. I tell the meditators to draw up a list of all their positive qualities, and it is surprising to me that in most of these lists there are many omissions, many things which are not there. So when I know someone well I mention more positive things to that person, and sometimes this really shocks and surprises them. There have been instances where people have come with about five or six positive things on their list, and I have added about ten or twelve to it!

This is very interesting. It shows what a strong conditioning, what a strong habit we have, that we mostly see only our minuses. It is a most unfortunate aspect of the human condition. It is everywhere, it is universal. I think I might have mentioned this: in South Africa, there was a teacher who teaches parents. And she told us that in one of the workshops for parents she asked them to draw up a list of all the bad things, wrong things, their children would do. Within a few minutes they could produce a long list! Then she asked: Now please draw up a list of the good things your children are doing. It was not easy for them. They had to think. They had to ask for ten more minutes to think about it!

"OK Meditation"

Here is another meditation: in fact, one day I gave you a guided meditation which I called "OK meditation". I got a few plusses for that guided OK meditation! You can apply it in everyday life, when you feel there is stress, anxiety, and so on, when you feel that you are very tired: "OK, OK." Just to say: "OK," and in that way to practice the OK meditation. Because please realise that it is resistance, it is dislike, it is not wanting, it is fighting, that is creating the tension, that is creating more stress. So this helps us to create some space, just spending a few minutes with the OK meditation. In a way it can also be seen as developing compassion, developing loving-kindness for what is happening. This is the beauty of loving-kindness: it is learning to make friends not only with very pleasant things, with beautiful things—that is easy. But this is the real challenge we have in everyday life, how to make friends with things that we do not like. It is by learning to say: "It is OK."

One day someone mentioned the non-reactive mind. I think before that we also had an exercise to see the difference between the reactive mind and the non-reactive mind. So this is another interesting tool to work with in everyday life, when difficult situations are arising, just to remember to think: How far can I not react to the stress?, How far can I not react to the anger that is arising?

Now, another tool that I have been emphasising very much is exploring, investigating, finding out. The ideal is: if stressful states of mind are arising, as they are arising, see if you can explore them, if you can investigate them, if you can find out, and make discoveries about them—if you can do this at that moment you get a hundred out of hundred—a big plus! But, most of the time you may not be able to do that because it is not easy.

14
INTEGRATING MEDITATION WITH EVERYDAY LIFE

Now I'm going to give a talk on how to integrate meditation with daily life. So please listen carefully with your complete attention.

We have to be clear about our priorities in life, we have to be clear where the practice of meditation figures in the list of priorities we have in life. If one is really prepared to make a commitment for the practice of meditation, that person will never say I don't have time to meditate. Please be clear on this point.

The second point, as we have been trying to do today and as I have been emphasising very much, is this very important aspect of just knowing what is happening in your mind and body, otherwise you are becoming more and more like a machine. Machines can function very efficiently but the machine does not know that it is functioning, it has no understanding, no knowledge. But knowing and understanding how our mind and body work is something we can do in everyday life. The things that we do habitually, mechanically, like brushing our teeth, combing our hair, dressing, all these small acts, little acts, please make an effort to do consciously, to know that you are doing them, to have your complete and full attention on them when you do those things.

Whether you are at home, whether you are travelling in a car, whether you are in your place of work, just to know, just to be aware of what is going through your mind and body from moment-to-moment as far as possible. It is the only way to integrate meditation with our daily life.

Another aspect that I emphasised here is our thoughts. During the day just be aware, just be conscious: What are the thoughts that I'm having? Are they about the past? Are they about the future? Are they about me? Are they about others? From the time we wake up to the time we go to sleep we have these continuous thoughts going through the mind, they never stop. We have to make an effort to learn about these things. By learning about your thoughts you can try to understand the type of person you are, you can gain self-knowledge, self-understanding. This is very important for the meditation.

Another problem in everyday life related to this is our emotions: unpleasant emotions that create suffering for us and create conflict for us. Unless we are meditators we really don't know how these emotions are created. What happens to people is that they *suffer* from these emotions and they don't know why they are suffering, and so they continue to suffer in this world. If you can understand the mechanism, the relationship, the conditions that create these emotions, how they are directly related to thoughts, then you can work with them, you can make them the objects of meditation.

INVESTIGATING OUR LIKES AND DISLIKES

Another aspect that I have been emphasising, and it is very important in everyday life, is to find out what is unpleasant for you, what is disturbing you, what is bothering you, and to make that the object of meditation. You might remember today when we were meditating we heard some big noise outside. At that stage I suggested to you, let us listen to that sound. I suggested we could listen to it as if for the first time; otherwise we will consider it as a noise, we will consider it as a disturbance, we might get angry, we will suffer as a result of that noise outside. When we learn to make that the object of meditation we can learn from any situation, any experience in life.

The same thing applies to people we have problems with. This is one of the greatest challenges we have in everyday life: relationships. You have to have relationships with people at home, you have to have relationships with people at the place of work. We cannot move away from relationships.

Let us take the case of someone in everyday life making your life miserable, creating problems for you, creating suffering for you. An interesting way of relating to such a person is to relate to them as your teacher, as your guru. Learn to use that person to observe your own mind, to see your own reactions to that person. Then you realise that the problem is not with that other person but how you are relating to him, how you are reacting to that person.

This is the beauty of the Buddha's teaching. If the suffering is outside, we can never free ourselves from suffering. But because we are creating our own suffering then we can free ourselves of the suffering. Sometimes I define meditation as finding the medicine for the sickness that we create ourselves. So, as we create the sickness, we have to discover the medicine. Once we have discovered that meditation is the medicine, we have to use it, we have to apply it in everyday life. And sometimes, as you know, medicine can be very unpleasant; it is not always sweet, not always nice. But if you want to cure yourself, even if it is not pleasant you have to take the medicine. So these unpleasant experiences we have—physical pain, mental pain—they are unpleasant, certainly, but as I have been saying, we have to learn from them, they have to be our object of meditation.

Consumerism

Another challenge you have in everyday life is materialism, consumerism. When you live in a rich country like this, you cannot separate, you don't know, it's not clear, what you really need and what is simply your greed. The society you live in can create desires in you, needs in you, which are not really necessary. A very important aspect of meditation in everyday life is learning to lead a simple life. It is something very beautiful to be simple, learning to be simple in our way of living. So when there is an urge or when there is a need to buy things, when you see the things you should ask: Now is this really necessary for me? Why do I really need this? Is it because other people are wearing this or other people are using that or do I really need it?

So you need to really ask that question when living in a consumer society. Then you'll realise your joy, your happiness, your lightness come not from external things, not from goods, not from what you possess, not from what you buy, but from something that comes from within yourself. This is the beauty of meditation. The need for external things drops away because you have become independent of external things. They drop away. And as I said, joy and lightness come from within yourself.

LOVING-KINDNESS

Another very important meditation, especially when practised in everyday life, is meditation on loving-kindness. One aspect of loving-kindness is learning to be your own best friend. If you can really make that connection with yourself you'll never do things which are unskilful for you, unwholesome for you, which create your own suffering and suffering for others. And it is only when you are friendly to yourself that you can really be friendly to others.

First we have to open our hearts to ourselves, then we can open our hearts to others. There are many aspects of loving-kindness; in fact I gave a talk on this subject, and on that day we distributed a booklet on loving-kindness, so please read it. But I would like to just mention two aspects of loving-kindness: one is forgiveness and the other is feeling grateful.

In everyday life we need to forgive ourselves and to forgive others. If we cannot forgive ourselves and forgive others then what happens is that we can be holding on to certain experiences, certain wounds that have been created, and this can create a lot of suffering for ourselves in everyday life.

As we are human we are bound to make mistakes. But when you make mistakes, there is no need to suffer and no need to feel guilty and beat yourself for having made mistakes; rather learn to forgive yourself and learn from these mistakes. And other human beings, as they are also human, as they are also imperfect, they are also bound to make mistakes. If you cannot forgive other people what happens is that you are holding onto hatred and ill-will, which is very unwholesome for you.

When we develop more and more friendliness to others, more and more friendliness to ourselves, and more and more forgiveness to others and ourselves, then we learn to be kind to others, we learn to have loving-kindness in our relationships with others. There are so many human beings who are suffering unnecessarily. So when you see human beings suffering you should try to relate to them with gentleness, with kindness, sometimes smiling with them, sometimes doing a kind act which can make such a difference to them and you. And if you can really open up to loving-kindness you'll see so many opportunities in life, in society, where you can act in such a way, and this can generate lots of happiness for you and happiness for others.

Gratitude

Another very important quality I mentioned in relation to loving-kindness is this quality of feeling grateful. Before coming here I spent some time in India and while I was in the place where the Buddha became enlightened I was reflecting on what the Buddha did after his enlightenment. According to the tradition, after he became enlightened he spent seven days just looking at the tree which gave him shelter. Just reflect on this: Buddha spending seven days showing his gratitude for a tree. That shows what a very important quality feeling grateful is.

Do we feel grateful for things? Do we feel grateful for other people? Do you feel grateful that you have discovered the Dhamma, that you have a group of spiritual friends? Do we ever make an effort to develop this quality of feeling grateful? Do we ever feel grateful that we can see? There are people who cannot see. Do you feel grateful that you can hear? There are some people who cannot hear. Do you feel grateful that you are healthy and that you can practise meditation without any problem?

These are small things, little things, which we take for granted. You should visit very poor countries like India and Sri Lanka and then you might realise that you should feel grateful for some of the things you enjoy in this country. But do we ever think about this? In those countries there are people without food. So shouldn't we feel grateful when we have food to eat? There is another aspect of feeling grateful: as I said earlier in the discussion, when we have unpleasant experiences we should also feel grateful for them because we can learn from them, they become our teachers.

GRATITUDE FOR THE DHAMMA

Another aspect of meditation in everyday life is to have spiritual friends around you. I'm very happy that you have some groups here so that you can go to these groups and can spend some time with others, meditate with them and discuss with them. So feel grateful that you are a group of spiritual friends helping each other.

When you practise in this way in everyday life you can really see the result, you can see that the medicine the Buddha has given us really heals, it really works. Then you have more and more faith, more and more confidence in the medicine. And you have more and more confidence in yourself. Then you really feel grateful for the Buddha who discovered this medicine, and you feel happy that you have discovered it and that you are using it and you are feeling the result.

And what is beautiful about the Buddha's medicine is that it can be applied in any situation in life. It can be applied when you are sick. It can be applied when you encounter death in any way. It can be applied when we are hurt, frustrated, disappointed. It can be applied when we have very serious problems, very serious conflicts.

The only thing is, as I said in the beginning, that one has to be very clear about the practice. Are you really making a commitment to your practice? Have you really made a commitment to take the medicine? I think it is also important that while you are taking the medicine you should also encourage others to take the medicine by just sharing with them—this is what I am doing. Please see for yourselves.

Some of the suggestions I have been making so far about integrating meditation with daily life, are they too difficult, are they unreasonable, are they not within your reach? Buddha never said anything which normal human beings cannot do. The only thing you have to be sure about is to have a clear understanding of the teachings and to know how to apply them in different situations in life. This is the point that I am emphasising.

I don't think there is any need for me to say anything more. So I would like you to now just spend some time reflecting on some of the things that I have been mentioning. This kind of reflection is also a very important meditation. Just reflect on a particular theme which will help you and which will help others. This helps us to look at ourselves, to find out where we really stand in life. It helps us to find out whether we are really wasting our life.

According to the Buddha's teaching, to get a human birth is something very precious. But are we really making use of the preciousness of human birth? In what way can we use this preciousness? Let us reflect on this very important theme for a few minutes. And in reflecting on that, we can make a determination: Now, from today onwards, I'm making a real determination to take the medicine and free myself from the suffering that I create myself. And also an aspiration: Let me also get opportunities so that I can share the medicine with others, and by doing that I can make others happy.

So let us close our eyes and really reflect on this. May you continue to use the medicine and free yourself from the sickness that you create yourself.

* * *

DISCUSSION

Though there are different meditation techniques the principles are the same. I present different techniques because people have different temperaments. What I try to do is to relate to the meditators individually and find out what technique is more suitable for them.

Before we speak about the techniques we should be clear why we meditate. The purpose of meditation is to free ourselves from suffering. The Buddha often said: I teach the fact of suffering and the way out of suffering. So our purpose is to really to achieve a mind that is free and a heart that is boundless. And the techniques are rather simple but we complicate them because of the complicated minds we have. Human beings are very clever at complicating simple things! I often ask the question: What have human beings not complicated in life?

MEDITATION ON BREATHING

One of the techniques we presented was focusing on the breathing. Any difficulty about this technique?

Retreatant: When I observe the breathing I find that my mind is not calm and the breathing is fast.

Godwin: First I will say something about this technique. For whatever question you have, perhaps what I will say might cover it. The simple thing about this technique is that it is learning just to be aware. We try not only to learn about awareness in relation to breathing but to whatever is happening in our mind and body.

It is very simple: if you are having thoughts you just know that thoughts are there. If the breathing goes fast you know now the breathing is fast. If you have unpleasant sensations in the body, you know there are unpleasant sensations in the body. So, as I have been emphasising, the whole focus of the technique is *just knowing* what is happening from moment to moment. If your mind is calm, you know the mind is calm. If the mind is not calm, you know the mind is not calm.

If we are meditating to achieve a mind that is calm, then when calm comes we will hold onto the calm. This is how suffering is created. And so if there is calm there is also suffering. What this meditation aims at is something very simple: knowing what is happening; and as I have been saying very often, just being friendly and saying OK to whatever is happening. And if you can meditate in this way, at the time you are meditating you are free from suffering.

And what is also important is to use the breath not only when we are sitting. This is why I have been saying: please make a connection with your breath. So in everyday life at different moments you can just come back to your breath. The breath is our friend, it will help us to just experience the present moment, the *here* and the *now*. The idea is to sit and develop awareness, and then to use that awareness at other times. I would consider that to be more important than what is happening only when you are sitting, because it is in everyday life that suffering is created, problems are created and you have to face challenges.

Some meditators ask me: "Am I doing it right? How do I know whether I am progressing in my practice?" I tell them the progress is not what is happening when you are sitting but how you relate it to everyday life. In Sri Lanka we have very rich people who are sometimes very unkind to their servants. When they are learning meditation I tell them the way to know their progress is to see the way they are treating their servants at home. They are not very happy to hear such things!

So please realise our progress is in how we are relating in everyday life. It is a way of living. It is an art of living. It is a way of thinking. It is a matter of having a certain attitude towards life, like the story I related about the wise old Chinese man. So please see this clearly, please realise this. Perhaps, after I go over the techniques, I might go over with you that aspect of everyday living. Please don't associate meditation only with a particular posture, a particular time, a particular technique.

LOVING-KINDNESS

Another technique I presented was meditation on loving-kindness which I emphasise very much. And meditation on loving-kindness is related to all the techniques, because if you can learn to make friends with whatever is happening, in that moment there is freedom. The simple fact is that suffering comes when we resist something, whether in meditation or whether in everyday life. Loving-kindness, friendliness, gentleness, openness, allows us not to resist but just to flow with, just to be open to what is happening.

Anyway, any problems about meditation on loving-kindness? It's a funny question: Any problems about loving-kindness meditation!

Retreatant: Sometimes you may treat other people with loving-kindness, but other people may not treat you with loving-kindness, so what can we do about that?

Godwin: Very good question. This is what happens in everyday life. This is one of the greatest challenges we have in everyday life. People who are unfriendly to you, people who are unkind to you, people who are unreasonable towards you; they should be our gurus, they should be our masters, they should be our teachers. As one of my friends put it, they really present you with a mirror. So when you meet such people you should be really grateful for them because they are testing you.

The important thing is not to be concerned about what they are doing but to watch what is happening in your own mind. This is why we have been emphasising so much the practice of awareness, just knowing what is happening. Then, when you realise that the problem is what is happening here in your own mind and not what is happening out there, people may behave in any way but there is no reaction to that.

And as I have been emphasising, this shows that we are all still human. According to the Buddha, until and unless we are enlightened we are all crazy. We are living in a crazy world, but the problem with us is that we are taking these crazy people too seriously! The sane way to live in a crazy society is to realise this, to understand this and to have compassion towards the crazy people we have to be with. This is how we can relate to such people—they should be our teachers. So I hope you meet more and more such masters, such teachers, such gurus in your life, because they are much better for you than this so-called teacher from Sri Lanka! Any other questions about loving-kindness?

Awareness of Emotions

Retreatant: Sometimes I feel that someone has done something wrong, for example in the office I see people wasting paper, so I get a bit angry with them although I understand that they may be ignorant about this, but still the anger is there.

Godwin: It is interesting for me the example you gave. In Sri Lanka people get angry when others waste their food because food is such a precious, important thing. It is interesting that you get angry when you see people wasting paper! Now how does a meditator use such a situation? One way of working with such a situation is to watch your own reactions. Are you angry? Are you annoyed? Are you irritated? In what way are you reacting to that?

Sometimes it is interesting to experiment with it. One day you go in and you see such people and you watch: now how long will the anger last? Half an hour? One hour? Because of some paper? So you should look out for such people and see how you are reacting to such situations. Then that becomes a learning experience for you.

Now this doesn't mean that meditators are always passive, looking only at themselves. There are two very important words: reaction and response. Reaction is an emotional reaction to such a situation. Response is doing something meaningful, doing something creative without reacting emotionally. So you can have a kind of dialogue with such people in a very friendly, open way, trying to understand their behaviour. But it should be done in a very skilful way rather than speaking in a very angry way, in a judgmental way, as if you are thinking you are right and these people are wrong. Naturally there is a hostile reaction to that.

We should never be self-righteous in our life. When you see the mistakes of other people, without being self-righteous sometimes you can say to yourself: "I may not have made that mistake, but I may be making worse mistakes, having wrong thoughts in my mind." Then when you see wrong-doings you relate to human frailties in an entirely different way.

So it is good to have a dialogue with such people and just get them to reflect on what is happening to them. This may work, this may not work. If it works it's fine; and if it doesn't work, you should be able to see such human frailties and just understand that this is the way things are. So I would like to again emphasise the importance of getting the person to see what he or she is doing, to get that person to reflect as far as possible by asking questions, rather than imposing your opinion on other people.

And I would also like to suggest that in such situations, without being self-righteous, to honestly tell such persons: "I'm sure I have shortcomings in me and I'm full of imperfections because I'm still not an enlightened person, but I'm curious to know what makes you do this?" That can touch people very deeply rather than stating it in a self-righteous way.

MEDITATION WITHOUT AN OBJECT

Another technique that we practised which is very important, I feel, is what is called *objectless meditation*. Once you are established in awareness and you are stable in your mind, then you are in a position to allow anything to arise; you allow any thought to arise, allow any emotion to arise, especially emotions you don't like, any sensations to arise, and you learn just to observe, just to be with whatever is happening in that spacious mind.

This is a very useful meditation in everyday life. Then, in different situations, just to know what thoughts you are having, just to know what emotions you are having, just to know what sensations you are having, seeing what they are and learning not to react to them, making them the objects of meditation, making them learning experiences. So in everyday life when you are having an emotion like anger, fear, stress, you learn to make that an object of meditation. Meditation has different levels but to a great extent we should try to integrate it with everyday life. This is why we had one full day to work with emotions, and another full day to work with thoughts, because these are the two aspects, the two areas, that we have to deal with in everyday life. Any question about this practice?

❧ **Retreatant:** Regarding the objectless meditation, practically, how can we create a spacious mind in order to do such meditation?

❀ **Godwin:** Using a technique like focusing on breathing, we learn to develop awareness, we learn to develop a non-reactive mind, we learn to be open. Once you know that now you are fairly stable then you can open up to whatever is happening. And what is beautiful in this technique is that even when there are times when you don't have a spacious mind and when you are reacting, when you have some emotion, then that becomes an object of meditation, you learn about it, you investigate it. If you are unable to do it at that time when it will not be very easy, at least later on you can reflect on what happened and can learn from it.

Our mistakes, our failures, they're used as our teachers, they're used for our spiritual growth. It is a very beautiful way to live. Usually when we make a mistake we give ourselves a big minus, we feel guilty, we suffer from anger, all different reactions. But in this way there is no need to have such reactions to our mistakes, instead you learn about what happened to you, so this develops self-knowledge and you feel grateful for these emotions and reactions that you have had.

I would like to emphasise this very much because I know in this culture there's lots of suffering as a result of our failures, our mistakes. So hereafter please don't suffer as a result of them, make them the object of meditation, make an effort to learn from them, because we can use them as a mirror showing us where we are. Please be very clear on this point. Then you come to a state that whether these unpleasant emotions are there, or whether there are pleasant emotions, it makes no difference. No big plus when pleasant experiences are there, and no big minus when unpleasant experiences are there. As the Buddha said: We learn to see things just as they are.

MEDITATING ON PAIN

Retreatant: You taught us not to fight with our thoughts in everyday life, and particularly during meditation we should not fight against all the sensations. During meditation I find after sitting for about half an hour my legs become so painful that I have to put all my attention on the pain and it's like putting up a fight with those sensations. And if I try to accept the sensations then all my attention is on how to accept those sensations and therefore I have no room to do any observation of the thoughts.

So I would like to know when I should make a decision to change my posture, because I do not want to change my posture too often in case I might have to go through the pain in order to improve the sitting. It confuses me because I have to make a decision sometimes and I do not know what decision I should make.

Godwin: A few points. One is that working with pain is a very useful experience in meditation. In everyday life when we experience physical pain, what do we do? We try to do something about it immediately, change the posture or whatever, and then get rid of the pain because it is unpleasant. But by doing this we never learn about pain, which is a most important part of the human condition. We don't know what types of pain we might have to experience in the future, and this is why I have been repeating so often, meditation is learning to be open to unpleasant experiences. Please don't see them as a disturbance or a distraction. So this is one point.

Nothing is more important than the pain itself, either thoughts or whatever else, because that is what you are experiencing. Feel grateful for the pain because you can learn about the pain in a meditative situation. We have to avoid two extremes. One extreme is always saying yes to the body. This is pampering the body. Is there lots of pampering of the body in this country? A good question to reflect on. The body says: I want it. We immediately go for it because it is all available here. So it is very important to learn to say No sometimes. Saying Yes always is pampering. Always saying No is being too hard on ourselves. So it is very important to have the correct balance: when to say Yes, when to say No.

Now in relation to physical pain when you are meditating, if you immediately change the posture I would say that is pampering; and going through the pain, trying not to change the posture, grinding your teeth, enduring the pain, I would say that is the other extreme. So the middle way is learning, experimenting, exploring the pain, and then when it's unbearable change the posture, stand up: very simple.

Retreatant: I think it is rather difficult to know what is the point at which you have to be strict with yourself.

Godwin: Just play with it, just experiment with it, it's not as critical as you think. Don't be so serious about the practice. Yesterday you were speaking of people being like stones. This is the result if you are too serious and this is why I'm emphasising lightness, joy, experimenting, playing with meditation.

I think this brings up another aspect of meditation which I would like to mention. I think again that this is related to this culture, that people are very goal-oriented, they want to achieve results. It is very interesting that in everyday life you have goals to achieve, results to achieve, and you chase after goals even when you are meditating!

So naturally you go through the same stress, the same anxiety, the same tension, the same restlessness because you want to achieve some goals, some results. Buddha has something very interesting to say in this connection. He gave a simile. He said meditation is like being a gardener; so like a gardener you are enjoying planting the trees, vegetables and flowers, and the gardener is not bothered when the flowers will come, when the fruits will come but is enjoying what he is doing.

I have thought of a similar simile. The simile is trying to reach the top of a mountain which you are climbing. If you are concerned, if you are pre-occupied by what you are going to see when you reach the top, you'll miss the fun while climbing. While you are climbing, what is happening to you—the falls, the adventures, the problems—those become the practice, and don't be concerned about what will be there when you have reached the top. What is happening now is the practice, and not what is going to happen later on. So it doesn't matter whether they are pleasant experiences or unpleasant experiences, see them as practice. *That's* the practice, not getting rid of them.

THE IMPORTANCE OF REFLECTION

I would also like to make it clear now that from what I have been saying so far you might have the impression that meditation is only practising techniques. But there is also a very important area which I presented on a few occasions here, learning to reflect, learning to contemplate. This is very important, especially for our behaviour. To reflect in a very friendly, gentle way about the way we behave, the words that we use, and so on. We can learn a great deal from this reflection in relation to the way we are behaving, the judgements we are making.

If we can develop this quality of reflection we can see the Dhamma in any experience in life; any experience can be a meditation. It can be a sickness, it can be some disappointment, it can be some frustration, it can be some happiness, it can be anything, but just learning to reflect, to contemplate, to understand, is very important.

In this connection I would like to suggest a technique which you can practise in everyday life. In the evening after work when you go back home, I know everyone who goes home is tired, but please try to recover from that by maybe taking a shower or something similar, and then just for a few minutes take your mind back and reflect on how you spent the day. From the time you woke up to the time of that reflection, just try to go over all the things. See now, how many times did I get angry during the day, what were the occasions when there was stress, were there situations when I lost control of my emotions? You are not doing this as if you were a judge, trying to beat yourself, but in a very friendly, gentle, understanding way, just going over what happened.

And what is more important is also to reflect on the times when such disturbances were not there. Reflect on the good things that you have done, the generous things you have done, the friendly things you have done, the nice words you have used. You should also include these. This is more important or at least equally important.

If you can be more open to these positive things you'll be surprised to know what a good person you are! This type of reflection will enable us to know more about ourselves, to know about our behaviour in a very objective, clear way and when you do this a natural transformation will come in your behaviour without you trying to do anything.

Meditation and Yoga

I think another thing we learned on this retreat is yoga. Please don't forget yoga in everyday life. You don't have to do one hour of yoga, but in the morning when you wake up just spend five minutes, ten minutes, doing some of these physical exercises and movements. It will really awaken you physically and mentally. In the evening when you go back home take a shower and do a few exercises, immediately there will be a recovery.

Please try to combine meditation with yoga because physically, and this is one of the things I like to mention, it is very important to relax the body. I find that sometimes, due to the way you meditate, I can see on your faces that you are not relaxed. As I said, you are too serious, too tense, you may be trying to achieve something. When the body is relaxed the mind becomes relaxed, then both the mind and body are relaxed and you can meditate in a very relaxed, easy way.

And talking to some of the meditators here I find that they are mostly in their heads and not in their body so much. It is very important to make a connection with the body, feel the body, learn to listen to our body, to come back to the body as often as possible.

Retreatant: The thing I observed when doing yoga is the question of ownership, this concept of the self, because I found the body acts very independently. It would not always do things the way I want. I want to do postures like the yoga teacher but I can't do it. It is not up to me, the body has its independence.

Godwin: It is a very good point to realise our limitations and then, as you rightly said, realise we have no control. If we are the masters, we can say: "Do this, the body should behave like this," but we can't say that. This is why we have to learn to surrender to what is happening. This is why on one occasion I said we have to be open to uncertainty, because we have no control over what is happening in our mind and body and in the environment and in life.

Retreatant: I don't quite agree, because even with the yoga teacher when he first started, it can't be that he could do all the postures he can do now, so you have to gradually learn with your body.

Godwin: That's true, but it doesn't mean that he can say: "Now body, don't fall sick, don't die, please don't have white hair like Godwin's hair!" Even the Buddha could not control completely what happened to his body. The Buddha's body became sick, the Buddha's body became old, the Buddha's body died. The only difference was that whatever happened in the body it caused no suffering for him because he was not identifying himself with it.

DEVELOPING SENSITIVITY

Retreatant: Sometimes when we are meditating we have vibration or movement in the body? What should we do?

Godwin: Sometimes just allow the body to move. Sometimes you need to control it, to say: "Now stop it." The only thing is you should not react to it and say: "This is a funny feeling, this is strange, am I doing it right?" That is unnecessary. When we meditate so many things happen in our mind and body, but whatever happens, we're just learning to be aware, learning to say OK.

Retreatant: You told us that we should hear and see things when we go outside. I would like you to tell us more about how we see things.

Godwin: Normally when we see things our complete attention is not there. So what we can do, and this is what is sometimes very useful about nature, is that we can cultivate this way of looking at things by examining something very clearly, very closely, and at that time your whole attention, your whole awareness, is on that object that you are seeing.

If we can learn to do this in relation to seeing, our senses are really awakened. There's a freshness that arises, there is lightness in your being. I think as children we had this quality, but maybe with our pre-occupations, with our anxieties, with our thoughts, since they are there most of the time when we try to see things, with such a mind we hardly notice things. But when we develop this quality we can see small things, little things, much more clearly, so that these ordinary things can become extraordinary. In the Buddhist texts there are some very beautiful references to monks and nuns living in the forest and they describe very minutely what they hear, what they see.

Another word for this is to develop a kind of sensitivity in a positive sense to seeing things, hearing things, smelling things, feeling things, so your whole living is alive, is fresh, is new, is innocent. In the Dhammapada, a very important book in the Dhamma, it is said that if we do not cultivate this awareness, this alertness, we are like dead people. But we become alive with this quality.

I think that maybe you might have experienced this: before chanting, when we hear the sounds, how we can really make the sounds the object of meditation. If we can really hear them sharply, clearly, as if for the first time, then space is created in your mind only for the sounds; and the same quality of living can be present in whatever we do. When we are eating, we'll be really alive, we will be really conscious, really present when we are eating. This is what I'm trying to emphasise.

I would like to hear something about chanting. What is your experience with chanting?

Retreatant: I feel very irritated about the bell-ringing. It's very interesting sometimes when I concentrate on the chanting, it feels that the bell-ringing is very far away. But sometimes, I don't know when, I am still not so aware of my mind, sometimes the bell-ringing really gets very irritating to my brain, like something hitting me. I don't like it.

Godwin: Many experiences have both a plus and a minus, and this is why we have to say: "Now plus, now minus; now pleasant, now unpleasant—OK, this is life." So you see, chanting shows what life is. It doesn't go one way, it isn't all beautiful. You see how one can learn from anything. This is what I say, this is the way of life: pleasant things come, unpleasant things come. Can we be open to both?

I would like to share my thoughts about chanting. I love Chinese chanting. It really makes me—how shall I put it?—I feel I am really present. Sometimes without my knowledge, my body is moving: wonderful! And I like the bells because in Sri Lanka, we don't use bells, so it has some magic for me.

Retreatant: Actually the bell is a device to develop our awareness also, because the sound of the bell is very clear. Secondly, it vibrates slowly and reduces its volume to the end so your awareness can follow the bell from the time it is hit right to the end of it, when the sound finally vanishes.

Godwin: Very good point. Any more questions?

Making Your Own Discoveries

Retreatant: I still have one question. Talking about awareness, I want to know: during meditation I have many,

many imaginings. The imaginings keep coming. Is this one aspect of the nature of awareness? And even when I look at the clouds I see many, many things and so I want to know if imagination is a kind of thought?

❀ **Godwin:** Find out for yourself. This is what I have been encouraging people to do. When you imagine you can find out: "Now am I thinking? What is happening?" So tomorrow I would like you to experiment with it and come and share with me the discoveries you have made. This is what I have been trying to encourage. The last few days are for you to make your own discoveries. And if you learn to make your own discoveries, as I said on one occasion, when you leave this place, you will continue to make discoveries about life, about anything.

One danger about imagination is that you may not be able to be clear what is imagined and what is reality. I know some people have breakdowns because they don't know how to distinguish what is imagined and what is real. This is what is beautiful about the meditation techniques. There is nothing to imagine, it's something real, something objective, and then when there is unreality, imaginations, let them go, come back to the reality, such as sounds or sensations. When I meet people who have psychological problems, these are the techniques that I give them and for the first time they can distinguish between what is real and what is unreal.

I am very happy that you presented questions clarifying some problems and difficulties you have in meditation. I hope you are very clear about the medicine now. The important thing is to make a commitment to use the medicine in everyday life. I would like to urge you to really make use of the medicine; the medicine can really work and help you. You will see the medicine helps us to work with the sickness that we create ourselves. And I would also like to suggest that while you use the medicine yourself, please make an effort to share the medicine with others. There's a lot of people suffering in this world. So it is very important for us while we take the medicine to share it with others.

❧ **Retreatant:** I have a simple question: what is reality?

❀ **Godwin:** At the moment reality is just seeing, just hearing the sounds, just the breathing going on. After answering that profound question about what reality is, we can do some chanting.

15
THE IMPORTANCE OF AWARENESS

The subject of today's talk, as you know, is the importance of the practice of mindfulness, which is something very important for the practice of meditation. I am very happy to see some of you reading the little booklet we are bringing out today on the Satipaṭṭhāna Sutta which deals with the practice of mindfulness. It is also very nice to see some of you meditating.

Yesterday I suggested you make an effort to do some practice of mindfulness, so that what I'm going to say will make some sense in your own experience. If we do not practise mindfulness or awareness what will happen to us is that we will become more and more like machines. We will be doing things mechanically, habitually, repetitively, automatically. In this modern world there is such a lot of technology and machines that I think human beings are becoming more and more machine-like, like automatons. By doing this we are forgetting the real art of living.

And what is very unfortunate is that while human beings are becoming more and more like machines they are also losing a sense of the importance of feelings. So when human beings don't experience the very important aspect of feelings in themselves, then they cannot feel love for themselves, they cannot feel love for others, they cannot feel warmth for themselves, warmth for others. Perhaps that explains why there is such a lot of violence in the modern world as we become more and more violent towards ourselves, and more and more violent towards others. All this is related to an absence of awareness, to not knowing what is happening in our mind and body. This is the first point I want to make about the importance of mindfulness or awareness.

Experiencing the Present Moment

Another very important aspect of mindfulness is that it helps us to experience the present moment, the here and the now. It is funny to think that most of the time during the day we either live in the past, thinking about what has happened, or we live in the future, dwelling on what is going to happen. But the past and the future are not real—only the present is real. So it shows that human beings, because of their lack of awareness, are living in an unreal world which does not correspond to reality.

To make this clearer let me give an example of what is happening now. Physically you may be present here, you may even see me, but mentally you may be somewhere else completely. To be completely present, to know what I'm saying, you have to be here and now, in the present. Otherwise, as I said, physically you'll be present but mentally you'll be elsewhere. A meditation master described his practice as: When I eat, I eat; when I walk, I walk; when I sleep, I sleep. The words sound very simple but it means that he was, most of the time being, present with what he was doing.

An interesting question arises: what did he mean when he said when he sleeps, he sleeps? One interpretation of this is that even when we are asleep, with the dreams that we see we are in a way half awake, and we don't really experience deep sleep. However, for most of us when we are awake during the day, what happens? We are half-asleep! This is what we call living!

So if you really want to start living you have to develop this very important quality of being present, of being alert, of being awake. That is why the Buddha is called the Fully Awakened One. The whole practice of meditation and practice of mindfulness is a way of awakening our mind, awakening the Buddha-nature in us. And when we awaken the Buddha-nature within, the quality of living becomes so different.

Now please realise that being in the present doesn't mean that we don't have to use thoughts about the past and the future. Sometimes we have to plan about the future. If you did not plan about the future, you would not have come here. And if you forget the past you will not be able to go back to your home! So what is important for us is, through awareness, to see for ourselves how we are using the past and the future.

Psychologists say that sometimes depression and sadness are due to the way we are relating to the past, and that anxiety is due to the way we are relating to the future. With awareness, we need to understand how to use the past and the future consciously and deliberately, and then at other times we need to be present in the here and now.

Meditation as a Way of Living

Related to that is something which I'm going to emphasise very much and I consider very important. It is to use awareness in everyday life. Even with small things like brushing our teeth, combing our hair, drinking and eating. As I said earlier, we have become so used to doing these things we are like machines. But if you can really learn to practise awareness, mindfulness, in everyday life then meditation becomes a way of life.

I live in a lay meditation centre in Sri Lanka. What we emphasise in our centre is how to integrate daily life, your ordinary life, with meditation. Otherwise what happens is that daily life is one thing, meditation is another. So if you are really serious about the practice, meditation has to be a way of living. When you read the text that we are distributing today, the text which outlines the practice of awareness, you'll see that the Buddha is telling us to be mindful of most of the things that happen to us during the day.

You'll be surprised to read that the Buddha said that even when we are in the toilet, be mindful, be aware and be conscious of what is happening in the toilet. I call this the toilet meditation! Sometimes when I visit some rich homes, when I go to their toilets I see lots of books, magazines and things like that in the toilet. I would suggest that next time when you are in your toilet you'll experience such a difference if you can just be conscious, just be present while you are in the toilet.

Another very important aspect is eating. We work such a lot in order to eat, but do we really eat consciously? Is your awareness present while you are eating? Are you conscious of what you are tasting? Are you conscious of what you are chewing? Now chewing is a very important aspect. If you can make an effort to consciously chew your food you'll realise a difference when you are eating.

When you consider all this you'll realise that meditation is related to ordinary things, not extraordinary things, not special things. Some people have the wrong idea that meditation is about having some special experience, some extraordinary experience. But when you consider some of the meditation techniques, they are ordinary things, simple things like being aware of the breath, being conscious of walking, being aware of eating. So meditation is doing the simple, practical, ordinary things in life consciously, and then these ordinary things become extraordinary.

If you can learn to do these ordinary things with awareness, then you'll realise that even with ordinary things you can do them as if for the first time. When you look at others can you see them as if you are seeing them for the first time? Can you relate to yourself as if you are relating to yourself for the first time, without past images, without past judgements about yourself and others? Can you see a tree or flower or Buddha image as if for the first time? Please try that and you'll find that the quality of seeing is so different, it becomes so alive, it becomes so fresh, it becomes so innocent.

Awareness Leads to Insight

Another very important aspect of awareness is learning to explore, investigate with awareness, our unpleasant experiences. There is a beautiful simile which I like in one of the Buddhist texts. It compares awareness to a surgeon who is about to operate. The surgeon has to find out where to operate, where the wound is. To find that out, he has to investigate. Once he has investigated into what the problem is, then, with the surgeon's knife, he cuts it out, he heals it.

What the simile is saying is that with awareness we can find out, we can explore, we can investigate, we can discover the problem, and then with wisdom we can work with the problem that we have discovered. In everyday life we have problems like anger, anxiety, fears, sadness, guilt—all of these things really create suffering for us. As with the surgeon's investigation, we can find out, we can learn, we can discover, we can explore, we can experiment with such problems. And then, when you explore them, you'll realise that you yourself are creating the problem. And when you see that, you can use wisdom to free yourself from the problem. You can use wisdom to understand what is happening in your mind and body. Through this understanding you can bring about a change, or continue working with the problems, investigating them, exploring them. The unpleasant experience itself becomes an object of meditation.

So also please realise that meditation is not always about having pleasant, positive experiences. Actually unpleasant experiences do not create any problems for us unless we identify ourselves with them. The real challenge we have is learning how to work with these unpleasant experiences, how to work with physical pain, how to work with mental pain. This is much more important than simply experiencing pleasant, positive experiences.

* * *

Discussion

Retreatant: My question is: all human beings have many bad habits like gambling, womanising, drinking, smoking. How do we handle these bad habits?

Godwin: Very interesting list. Actually, one of the aspects of meditation is working with habits. What has happened to us is that we have become dependent on these habits. Then what happens is that we respond to these habits in a very mechanical way. The urge comes and then we just give in to it. So one suggestion I would like to offer—again this is very important in the practice of awareness—is just to know when these habits arise, to be conscious of them, to be aware of them so at least we can work with the mechanical aspect of these habits.

The second suggestion I would like to offer is to see for yourself how it creates suffering for yourself and how it can create suffering for others; and ask yourself does it give you joy, lightness and positive spiritual qualities?

The third suggestion is that when you are not experiencing these things, when you have not given in to these habits, just to see the difference when they are absent from your mind. Then you see in your own experience what it does to you when they are present and what it does to you when they are absent. Then they will naturally drop away on their own.

And as I said earlier, it is also very important to develop self-confidence: I know I have these habits but let me make a real effort to work with them. To make a real commitment, dedication, devotion to work with these habits can be something very useful.

And maybe the last suggestion is: it is helpful to associate with spiritual friends, noble friends. It is helpful to share your experiences with them and they can be also very supportive on the spiritual path you are following.

One last thought is: please don't feel guilty, don't feel bad, don't consider yourself as a sinner because you are doing these things. Don't see them as problems but see them as a challenge that you need to work with.

Part Three

THE IMPORTANCE OF THE BUDDHA'S TEACHINGS

16
THE FOUR NOBLE TRUTHS AND LIBERATION FROM SUFFERING

What we will try to do now is to explore together the Buddha's teaching about the Four Noble Truths, and to see how far we can apply them in our daily life, in our spiritual life; just using the teaching as a model to free ourselves.

The Four Noble Truths are as follows: the first is Suffering; the second is the Cause of Suffering; the third is Freedom; and the fourth is the Way to Achieve Freedom. Or another way of stating it is to use the medical model; then the truths are: Sickness, the Cause of Sickness, Health, and the Course of Medicine. So in meditation what we are trying to do is to use the medicine.

Now, the first question I would like to raise for discussion is: why did the Buddha call suffering a noble truth? How does suffering become a noble truth? What is so noble about suffering? It's because we have to *experience* suffering in order to feel the need to be free of it. Unless we know that we are sick, the need to take medicine will not arise. There are people who are sick, but they do not know that they are sick. Therefore the need to use the medicine, the need to find the medicine, does not arise. We deserve a big plus that we know: we know that there is a sickness and so then we are trying to discover the medicine and use it. So a big plus!

PHYSICAL AND MENTAL SUFFERING

Let us spend some time with this aspect of suffering. There is another word which is interesting: disease. It means that you are not at ease. So we will explore some areas, some aspects of suffering, or dis-ease, not being at ease. Yesterday we realised that having relationships is not always easy. I feel that this is the biggest disease. Certainly it is a very important area as we discovered yesterday. And it is useful to reflect why this is such a big disease. What are the other forms of disease in this world?

- **Retreatant:** Being hungry.

- **Godwin:** I am happy that you mentioned it because in Sri Lanka people know what it is to feel hungry. Here I do not think that there are opportunities to experience it. Am I right?

- **Retreatant:** I meant being mentally hungry.

- **Godwin:** That is nicely put: being mentally hungry. Now we can find out which is the greatest suffering, whether it is physical hunger or mental hunger. It is an interesting area to explore. I think some of you may not even be aware of some forms of poverty. Sometimes it is good to be exposed to other cultures and different situations. Then you will realise what a lot of—how shall I put it—abundance and consumerism there is here. I will just give an example: when you come to the West there are so many choices. I am always being asked: Do you like this tea or that one or another one, because there are so many varieties available.

One day I was taken by a friend of mine to have some ice cream, and there were about 30 varieties of ice cream! And I was asked to choose. I did not know how they would taste, so I just said: I would like this one. In Sri Lanka, no choices! In our Centre there are only limited choices, simple choices, like: do you drink water or do you drink tea? For breakfast there is only one meal. If you do not like it... That reminds me: there was once a Western monk staying there and I always used to say to people: "Try to eat the food here as if for the first time—that is a way of surviving here." But the monk said: "I eat it as if for the last time!"

Because of this affluence, in these affluent countries there is a disease which I call *affluenza*! Have you heard of this disease? It is very interesting to see the rest of the world suffering due to a lack of things, and here the suffering is due to affluence. I would like to say something about this on the last day also, because I feel this is something that it is important for you to reflect on. So this is one form of suffering. Anything else, any other forms of suffering?

Retreatant: There is suffering because of loneliness; and relationships are sometimes a cause of suffering.

Godwin: You speak of it as though from experience. It is quite true. Actually in Sri Lanka I sometimes meet both types of suffering: there are people who are single and alone, old and so on. This can really be a cause of suffering. Certainly when there is a war going on, such a lot of violence, tension, unrest around, it is not easy to live, it is not pleasant, or satisfactory.

There are these different types of suffering, but there is a very subtle kind of suffering that is presented in the Dhamma. Not to get what you want is certainly a source of suffering. But what is more subtle is that even to get what you want can also be a sort of suffering. Isn't it an important point for us to reflect upon? Here you have so many toys, even grown-ups have so many toys! And then you feel that were you to get this toy or that one then you would be happy, you would be content, you would be satisfied. Perhaps one toy is to travel around the world. You may be longing for that, and then you get it, but at the end of it there is nowhere else to go!

So this is why I said one has to have a deep sensitivity, a very deep sensitivity to be aware of these conditions, these situations. It shows that the dimension of suffering has so many facets, so many aspects. And it is interesting that the Buddha started with this. Suffering is a fact. It is a fact that every human being can experience, has experienced.

Accepting Responsibility

Now the second noble truth is not so easy, not so clear. Because there you are told that the cause of suffering is your own models, your own expectations, your own ideas, your own assumptions, your own desires, you own wanting things to be only your own way. This is the cause of suffering. I feel that the second noble truth is extremely important because only when you realise *that* can the third and the fourth noble truths follow. So we will spend a few minutes just reflecting on the implications of the second noble truth.

One point is that when you see this you have to take responsibility for what is happening inside yourself. This is not an easy teaching. To have complete self-reliance and to say: I create my own suffering and therefore only I can free myself. Because there are some easier teachings, where you are told: I will help you, you have only to trust or surrender to me and everything will be all right. You do not have to do anything, only have trust and have faith and believe and so on.

So this second noble truth is an extremely radical teaching, and it is not an easy teaching. What is also difficult and subtle is for you to fully realise this truth. Take the example I gave this morning: something that you consider as extremely precious, more precious than your life, and someone steals it. Then when you are suffering, when you are sad, someone asks you: "Why are you sad, why are you suffering?" You say: "That person took my most precious possession."

When we are angry sometimes we are asked: "Why are you angry?" We answer: "This person hurt me, this person did such and such to me, that is why I am angry." So you see the second noble truth is something very subtle to realise. When my precious possession has been stolen we say it is because this man stole it that I feel sad. But can I do something other than act like that? Can I let go of my identification with what I consider as something very precious? And then you realise there is no suffering, and this is a very hard medicine. And in fact, some medicines are not very pleasant, not very sweet. So this medicine that is presented is also not very easy.

Once I met a Tibetan monk who had been imprisoned by the Chinese security forces and I asked him: "Did you suffer when you were tortured? According to the Dhamma how do you see that?" Then he said: "I know that it was because these people were torturing me that I was suffering. But as a meditator I had been practising very hard with physical pain, sitting for 2 or 3 hours at a stretch. So when they were torturing me I was trying to see how far I could work with the pain rather than hate the person torturing me. I tried my best to use the Buddha's medicine when I was suffering. Sometimes I was very successful and I had real gratitude for the Buddha's teaching, I saw the medicine was working. And when the medicine was not working when I was suffering, I thought: May I be able to practice more."

I read a very moving instance, which is similar to this, but it was mentioned by a Christian priest. I do not know the details; he was being tortured in a prison to get a confession out of him. And he was quite calm, silent. Then the man who was torturing him said: "Why don't you speak, don't you know that I can kill you?" He answered: "Don't you realise that my body is already dead?" This is the medicine, it is difficult medicine, it is hard medicine. But it is based on an interesting principle.

Taking the Medicine

Now, I would like to say something about what we do with the medicine, because we are all here trying to take the medicine, trying to taste the medicine. But we can also be doing other very interesting things with the medicine. One thing is that without taking the medicine we can read all about the prescription. I know scholars in Sri Lanka—we have outstanding Buddhist scholars—and they know the medicine from A to Z. And when you listen to them, you feel that they have not really taken the medicine, but they have only spoken from books. I was a librarian and I also considered books as toys. This can be a trap, where you are accumulating knowledge about the prescription, about the medicine, and talking to others about the medicine, but you have never tasted the medicine yourself.

Then there are other types of people who like to give the medicine to others but they never take it themselves. They are the so-called meditation-teachers! They are very good in getting others to take the medicine, saying: It is wonderful, it is great, and so on.

You can see there are many traps to fall into—I will mention some more. Another is you take the medicine for some time and you realise nothing is happening so you try to change the medicine. Here in the West you have many medicines, sold in what I call spiritual supermarkets. You try one medicine for a few days. Maybe you see an advertisement and you go to try another medicine. You keep on changing them without really giving any of them a chance. Not really making a commitment to a particular medicine.

Then another thing some persons do is that they take the medicine only on meditation retreats. And they say: "In everyday life I cannot take the medicine. It is just impossible. So I am waiting for retreats to take the medicine." Then they do one retreat after the other! This is another way of taking the medicine.

Then there is another very subtle way of using the medicine, where you use the medicine to do just what you like to do. I will give one or two examples. One medicine that is offered is that you must learn to be kind to the body. So in everyday life you think: "Getting up at 6 o'clock for meditating is not very nice to the body, getting up at 8:30 or 9.00 is good enough." And what is dangerous is that you are using the medicine to do only what you like to do.

Another very dangerous medicine is that according to the second noble truth people create their own suffering, so I can do anything I like to others. That is a very dangerous medicine. The Buddha has warned against that. He said it is like catching hold of a poisonous snake at the wrong end. In a relationship a so-called meditator doing that can inflict suffering on another person, and then he says: "Are you suffering? You are creating it yourself. You hurt your own mind. I am just doing what I should be doing." Very easy! You see how complicated human beings are. The medicine is for healing yourself and for healing others. But here it is being used in a very destructive way. So once again one has to be very clear, one has to be very sensitive.

This brings up the importance of having spiritual friends around. You should be very grateful for the feedback you get from them, because we sometimes have what are called blind spots where we cannot see things clearly ourselves. But with all these difficulties, with all these blind spots, if you can really take the medicine, then you realise that the medicine is really helping you.

Results of Taking the Medicine

In practical terms what does it mean to say that the medicine is working? In simple terms it is where you realise your suffering is becoming less and less. Or to put it in more positive terms: you have more loving-kindness. Symptoms from the sickness will arise, as the monsters will arise, but you are very clear about the medicine and you have the confidence that the medicine is going to help you, because you know it through experience.

I am reluctant to speak about stages, but what I would like a meditator to achieve is such a state where he or she can say with complete self-confidence that the monsters will arise, but that there is no problem when they arise because they know the medicine that works. And then you come to a state where, whether the monsters come or whether the monsters do not come, makes no difference. Why? Because when they are there you know what to do. And when they are not there, you know that they are not there.

Another very important sign that the medicine is working is having loving-kindness towards other people. Then, when you see people suffering from the same sickness, and when you realise that the medicine is working for you, you engage with them and say: Please try this. I think this is a very important aspect in our practice, to be able to give to others, to be able to help others. I was very happy to hear from the yoga teacher that her own teacher in the morning would say: Now whom can I help today? You can ask the question during the whole day: How can I help other people? And then do it.

This is a very good medicine, because otherwise one of the dangers is that when you take to meditation, self-awareness, introspection, you become so preoccupied with yourself, you become so self-centred within yourself, you have no regard for the people around you. This can be another danger of the medicine. So it is extremely important while helping yourself to help others also. In fact, it is a very effective medicine because otherwise with our problems, with our suffering, with our wounds we can really be preoccupied with them, overwhelmed by them, and not having any regard, any concern, any sensitivity to others. In fact this is an effective way you can try to forget your worries, your concerns and see how far you can relate to another person.

I would just like to share an experience of a meditator at Nilambe. She had some deep wounds, deep problems. In isolation she was really being with them most of the time. Because this is really a meditation centre, a retreat centre, you have a lot of time by yourself. Then you can really be stuck in this inner world that you have created. So sometimes I encourage meditators to go and help people and to see the suffering of others. Because in Sri Lanka there are so many opportunities to see different forms of suffering. So she went to a place where there are retarded children, deformed children, and when she saw them with all their suffering her own suffering was forgotten and she forgot herself and picked them up and cared for them. There was an immense change in her.

I think I will stop now and if you have any questions, any disagreements, please present them: it is a very important theme.

Violence from Others

Retreatant: Can there be suffering because of the desire of others, for instance when someone sexually assaults another person?

Godwin: I am happy you mention sexual assault, because I have been trying to help some people who have been sexually abused and people who have been raped. I will share very briefly how the medicine can be given in this situation.

One thing I realised from the victims was that they were very angry about the person who was responsible for that incident. When I worked with them I did not tell them about the second noble truth. I told them: "Yes, you are suffering. All this has been created by the other person. I can understand your anger." As I said on a previous occasion I would tell them: "Please go somewhere and show your anger, express your anger, bring it out."

Another thing I experienced with them is that they feel guilty, because they feel responsible for what the other person did to them. Here again I would tell them: "It is natural that you feel guilty. But let us work slowly, gradually, gently to find out how far you can let go of the guilt." I do not tell them that the guilt is their own creation. I say: "It is okay that you feel guilty, but see how far you can forgive yourself." It is not easy and it takes some time, but slowly, slowly the medicine may start to help.

Another thing I realised is the way they related to their body. Because it has happened to their body they hate their body; and sometimes they feel alienated from their body, they feel as if it is another's body. So when they tell me: "Well, I feel as if this body is not mine", I do not say to them: "This is the Buddha's teaching, this body is not yours." I tell them: "It is natural that you should feel this way." And I have some exercises I give to people to work with the body. This is the beauty of the medicine, that it is so flexible, that it can be used in a very creative way, used where the person is. For such people I do not give a lecture on the Four Noble Truths!

17
THE IMPORTANCE OF THE DHAMMA IN THE MODERN WORLD

Most people believe that material things are important, that happiness lies in material things. In fact, the more material things you get, the more dissatisfied you are; and the more dissatisfied you are, the more material things you want to get! Buddha has given a very powerful simile to describe this condition. He compared it to a dog with a bone. The dog won't let go of the bone and is just holding on to it, and is still hungry and still dissatisfied, and still suffers from fear of losing that bone.

Related to this serious problem of materialism is another aspect, another manifestation of this, called consumerism. It's a real challenge for people to live in consumer societies and yet not be affected by the consumerism around them. Consumerism has many aspects, but I see two dangerous aspects in consumerism. One is that people are not clear about what they actually need and what is just their greed. According to the Dhamma we need certain things: food, clothing, shelter, and medicine—they are called the four requisites.

The four necessary things are things that human beings really need. So there's a place for material things, but then when they become our goals and when we are confused between greed and need, this is where they can lead to dissatisfaction and suffering.

Another dangerous aspect of consumerism is that the society that you live in starts manipulating you, and the danger is that you don't know that you are being manipulated. You become like puppets, puppets in the hands of a society that creates desire, creates greed, and this all leads to more and more frustration. So isn't this a sad situation when human beings have the potentiality of becoming free, of becoming enlightened? We have the Buddha-nature in us, but this aspect is not recognised and instead we become victims of the society that we live in.

ACQUISITIONS

The simile that has come to my mind about this situation is that though we are grown up we have become dependent on what I call toys. I'm interested to know what toys human beings go after in this culture, in this country. What I mean by toys are external things where you think you will find happiness, joy, and peace. You start acquiring toys, and then you change one toy for another, and your whole life is spent on getting toys and yet still you are dissatisfied. So can I hear from you some of the toys that you are interested in acquiring?

Retreatant: Shopping.

Retreatant: Housing.

Godwin: In a way houses are necessary, but then you are not satisfied with a small house, so the house becomes bigger and bigger, and then that can become a toy and you are still dissatisfied. You have a beautiful new house but you're not happy. Maybe you should move into a bigger house? That can be a problem.

Retreatant: Computers.

Godwin: Now that toy has even been introduced to Sri Lanka! Anyway we can draw up a long list of toys. An interesting question is: is meditation also a toy? Is there a relationship between these toys and meditation?

Retreatant: Yes.

Godwin: I would suggest that with meditation you become your own toy. This is the importance of the Dhamma. This is the importance of the Buddha's wonderful teaching. When you become your own toy you can be happy, contented, and peaceful with yourself. So the need for external toys, external things drops away because you find the joy and happiness from within.

BECOMING YOUR OWN BEST FRIEND

Another very important aspect of meditation is learning to enjoy your own company. When meditators come to the centre where I live in Sri Lanka, I tell them to spend some time alone and see what happens when they are alone with themselves. It's interesting. Some of the people who come there have never spent any time completely alone with themselves, without any toys. Then what happens? They become lonely, they become bored. What does it show about ourselves? We cannot stay with ourselves for more than 10 or 15 minutes and we want to escape from ourselves!

So the importance of the Dhamma is that you realise that, you work through that, and as I said, you learn to be your own best friend. You learn to be self-contained, contented with yourself. Such a person is described in the Dhamma as someone who is at home wherever he is. Such a person can be happy with himself while being alone, and such a person can be happy with others.

I would like to touch on another aspect which shows the importance of the Dhamma. With the practice of the Dhamma in all the situations you face in life, you come to see the Dhamma in any situation. As I said yesterday, even unpleasant experiences will become learning experiences.

I know in this culture that people are afraid to make mistakes because of the emphasis on wanting to be perfect. With this model of perfection, what happens is that when we make a mistake we beat ourselves, we hate ourselves, we lose our self-confidence, and we see ourselves as worthless. In my language, you see only minuses in yourself; and when you see minuses in yourself, you see minuses in others too, so that you can create a hell with only minuses.

The importance of the Dhamma here is that it enables us to not create suffering in this way because of our mistakes, but instead we learn to ask the question: what can I learn from my mistake? What does it indicate about myself? This kind of inquiry has to be done in a very friendly, gentle, understanding way, without giving any minuses. Then our mistakes themselves help us to grow in the spiritual path. Isn't that a beautiful way of living? Learning from your mistakes; and then when you see mistakes in others you also learn to relate to the mistakes of others in an entirely different way. So we learn to appreciate our humanness, not the idea of perfection. Then we learn to appreciate the humanness of others.

So the importance of the teaching is that we see clearly how we create our own suffering, and through that realisation it becomes clear that only we can free ourselves of the suffering we create ourselves. Then we become self-reliant. Then we learn to have self-confidence that whatever arises, I know how to handle it with the help of the Dhamma. Then you learn to be your own teacher. And as the Buddha said, you learn to be a light unto yourself.

One last point on this topic. I have had the good fortune to meet many masters, many gurus, many teachers from many traditions. Do you know which master, which guru has most inspired me? It is life itself. Life is our best teacher. So, thanks to the Dhamma, when you realise the importance of the Dhamma, life becomes your teacher. And sometimes life can be a very hard teacher, but it is always a good teacher. It can indicate to us what we really are.

Now I will stop and if you have any questions, please ask them. In the last few days you have been asking very good, practical questions relating to life, so I hope you will do so today also. I touched on some areas which are related to your life here, so please feel free to ask any questions and let us see how the Dhamma, how the Buddha's teachings can help us to work with these problems.

෴ **Retreatant:** I remember in the texts that the Buddha always taught his students to be their own island. Even when he was dying, the last lesson he gave his students was: be your own island. I think this bears a very direct similarity to what you told us. We always have to learn from ourselves.

❀ **Godwin:** Yes, and also, as I said, to learn from life. It means that as you live, if you are really sensitive and open, and if you are really practising the teaching, then you learn how to relate everything that happens to you in life, and in relations with others, to the teaching. Then all these experiences we have in life, they can be used for our spiritual growth. There's a teacher who said that they are compost! Compost contains things which are not considered useful, which are considered as dirty, and which we throw away. So all this rubbish, if we can collect it, it can be used for the growth of vegetables and fruits.

I would say that what we learn from life, even from our mistakes, can be seen as compost, that it can be used for our own spiritual growth. It's only then that, as the Buddha said, you can be an island to yourself, that you can rely on yourself. But what is important to note is that if you have the conclusion that you know everything, that is the end of learning. So it is very necessary to have this don't-know mind, whereby we can learn from anything and we can learn from anyone. This is something very important in the Buddha's teaching.

❦ **Retreatant:** How can we be our own toy and be satisfied with ourselves, how can we be our own best friends?

❀ **Godwin:** It is interesting that for different reasons we become our own enemies—and then we think that the enemy is outside ourselves! We are trying to find the enemy outside ourselves without realising the biggest enemy is inside ourselves. One aspect of being your enemy is, as I said, seeing only your mistakes, seeing only your shortcomings, seeing only your minuses. This can be a very self-destructive aspect where you become your own worst enemy.

Another aspect related to this point is that when you don't see the good side in yourself you don't see the good things that you have been doing. I meet many good people and they are following the spiritual path, but because of this tendency to be self-destructive they don't see their own worthiness, they don't see their own value, they refuse to see the Buddha-nature in themselves. When you realise this, that you are your own enemy, then you learn to work on this condition. This is the importance of awareness, which we discussed yesterday. So with awareness you catch yourself, you realise what you are doing to yourself, that you are becoming your own enemy.

And another point is this very beautiful meditation of loving-kindness. I emphasise this meditation very much. It is psychologically very interesting that meditation of loving-kindness begins with oneself. It shows that we cannot be friendly to others unless we are friendly to ourselves. Meditation on loving-kindness helps us to be our own best friend, it helps us to make a connection with ourselves.

Another thing about meditation on loving-kindness is this: it helps us to forgive ourselves. As I said earlier, to accept our humanness; and when we learn to accept our humanness, then we learn to accept the humanness of others. So it helps us to be friendly with ourselves and friendly to others.

Another aspect of being our own best friend is that we don't realise how we affect ourselves in an unwholesome, unskilful way with our attitudes and behaviour. But when you make this connection with yourself there is a change that takes place, a transformation takes place, so that whatever you do, your words and your thoughts will always be related to the skilful, the wholesome, what should be of help to you in your spiritual path.

Retreatant: I always feel bored when I'm alone. Can you tell us your actual experience of how you enjoy your life alone?

Godwin: To give a brief answer: When we are alone, when we feel lonely, when we feel bored, what we do when these states of mind arise, is that we give in to them, we try to change them by doing something. So the simple answer is, hereafter when you have loneliness, when you have boredom, don't try to escape from it, go through the loneliness, go through the boredom. Yesterday I said a very important aspect of meditation is learning to go through unpleasant experiences, whether physical or mental. In the beginning it will be very unpleasant, but this shows the importance of the practice. You have to go through the unpleasant experience and then from loneliness you move on to experience what is aloneness, which is entirely different from loneliness, thereby learning to enjoy your own company.

THE SIMILE OF THE LOTUS

Retreatant: You warned us of the dangers of consumerism and materialism. Obviously this requires a certain renunciation of those things. Could you give us some advice on how to begin the renunciation so it's not all at once and such an overpowering obstacle?

Godwin: As I said, this is one of the greatest challenges we have: how to live in a materialistic society where there is such consumerism and still not be affected by it. So I'll try to offer some practical suggestions. One suggestion that I would like to offer is that when you see things which you think you need—again this shows the importance of awareness—to catch yourself and to ask the question: "Do I really need it?" And ask the very profound question: "Why do I need this?" When this obsession to possess something comes we never ask the question: "Do I really need it? Why am I needing it?"

When you are living in a consumer society and when you raise this question, you realise that it is because others are using these things, and because others are using them you want to be like them. So without your knowledge you get caught in the rat-race, then your whole life becomes a competition, competing with others.

Another practical suggestion I would like to offer is to learn to say Yes to some things; and to learn to say No to certain other things. What happens to us is that due to different reasons we have got used to pampering ourselves. Pampering is always saying Yes to whatever the body or the mind wants. What is important in the practice is both finding out that you're pampering yourself, and then to say No in a very gentle friendly way. It is very important in life, learning to say No to certain things. This is the only way to work with the things that we have become dependent on.

The third suggestion I would like to offer is in a way an indirect one. With more and more practice, when you have learnt to be your own best friend, when you have made a connection with yourself, then naturally you don't have to make an effort at renunciation. You can live in a consumer society but you are not affected by the environment. In this connection there is a beautiful Buddhist symbol. The Buddhist symbol is being like a lotus. Where does the lotus grow? In muddy water. Now the lotus flower is able to grow in that muddy water without being affected by the muddy water around it. So this is the importance of the Buddha's teaching, that when you live within society, within that environment, you will be able to steady your way and not be affected by what is happening externally because a shift has been taking place inside you.

* * *

Of Related Interest

JUST SEEING
Insight Meditation and Sense-Perception
By Cynthia Thatcher

In eloquent, expressive language this book explores in depth the Buddha's significant teaching, "When seeing, just see; when hearing, just hear," as it applies to the practice of insight meditation as taught by Mahasi Sayadaw. Along the way, the book touches on the two kinds of reality—ultimate and conventional—expounded in the Abhidhamma. The author explains these two realities through the example of a pointillist painting of Seurat that can be viewed in two ways. In addition, there are meditation instructions for beginners, an appendix on the perceptual process as described in Buddhist metaphysics, and a crossword puzzle of Pali terms.

BP 505S   146 pp.

MEDITATION
Talks on Meditation
Ajahn Chah

This compilation consists of five talks and three question and answer sessions by the renowned Thai Forest Tradition teacher Venerable Ajahn Chah. The selected talks mainly deal with the topic of meditation, both tranquillity meditation as well as insight meditation. Ajahn Chah discusses the beginning steps as well as the higher stages and this book is a source of inspiration for beginners as well as serious practitioners.

BP 519S   158 pp.

WITHIN OUR OWN HEARTS
Ayyā Khemā

This inspiring book is based on twelve talks that the well-known female meditation teacher gave at her meditation centre in Sri Lanka. Ayyā Khemā, born in Germany, insists that the Buddha's teachings, though profound, are simple and can be realized within our own hearts.

BP 518S   124 pp.

All prices as in the latest BPS catalogue (http://www.bps.lk)

THE BUDDHIST PUBLICATION SOCIETY

The BPS is an approved charity dedicated to making known the Teaching of the Buddha, which has a vital message for all people.

Founded in 1958, the BPS has published a wide variety of books and booklets covering a great range of topics. Its publications include accurate annotated translations of the Buddha's discourses, standard reference works, as well as original contemporary expositions of Buddhist thought and practice. These works present Buddhism as it truly is—a dynamic force which has influenced receptive minds for the past 2500 years and is still as relevant today as it was when it first arose.

For more information about the BPS and our publications, please visit our website, or write an e-mail, or a letter to the:

Administrative Secretary
Buddhist Publication Society
P.O. Box 61
54 Sangharaja Mawatha
Kandy • Sri Lanka
E-mail: bps@bps.lk
web site: http://www.bps.lk
Tel: 0094 81 223 7283 • Fax: 0094 81 222 3679